Mrs Miller's Gift

The Story of Edinburgh Psychic College and Library

later renamed

Edinburgh College of Parapsychology

in celebration of its 75th Anniversary,
8th September 2007

by

Gerald O'Hara B.Sc
&
Ann Harrison B.Educ.

Published by
Saturday Night Press Publications
York, England
snppbooks@yahoo.co.uk

for contact with
Edinburgh College of Parapsychology
info@parapsychology.org.uk

www.parapsychology.org.uk

ISBN 978-0-9514534-9-0

Printed by Lightning Source
www.lightningsource.com

Cover photo:- 30 Heriot Row, Ediburgh in 2007

Dedicated to....

all those people named and unnamed, known and unknown, who throughout the changing times which the last 75 years have brought, have served, supported and worked in whatever way they could, in many cases have devoted their lives, to keep this Gift alive and well for all those who come in search of Knowledge - whether from this side of life or the other.

Acknowledgements

Without the enterprising outlook and untiring support of Principal Magnus McInnes and his wife Angela, this book would never have been written. They had the vision to see that the College of Parapsychology archives would be the source of an interesting and important story.

May we offer thanks for additional material to Alf and June Winchester, Major Bob Findlay, Mary Armour, Nita Saunders, Weilda White, Carole Lynne, Rosalind Cattanach, Jean Bassett, Raymond Smith and secretary George Cornick.

Special thanks go to Stewart Alexander and Ray Taylor, editor Psychic World, for permission to use various articles from Psychic World and illustrations from the Helen Duncan book by Alan Crossley.

Thanks also to Paul Gaunt at the Psychicpioneer website for his help with information about Colin Evans and various illustrations; to editor Tony Ortzen and staff of Psychic News for permission to use their photographs.

For when our eyes and minds were too close to the words we had written, our thanks go to Jane Jackson and Sharon Cartmel for their untiring proof reading.

We gratefully acknowledge all the information gleaned from numerous books whose authors and publishers we have been unable to trace - your words have added colour to our story.

Finally, thanks to Stephanie and Graham for the use of their holiday home in Argyll - a haven of peace for Gerald's writing and research.

Contents

Foreword

I feel so fortunate to have been part of the Edinburgh College of Parapsychology and I know that my wife, Angela, feels the same. Because of its independent standing the College has had the freedom to bring the work of the Spirit closer to the people of Edinburgh. In recent years, standards have improved and these improvements have been consolidated in the work of the College. We have nurtured many students some of whom have developed as speakers and teachers. Numerous lives have been enriched by association with the College and I know that it has given many people strength and courage to carry on.

There has also been great change in the structure and running of the College and a diversification, with progress towards more openness and accessibility. As a result of this there has been a good response from the public. The programme today covers a wide range of psychic investigation with workshops, lectures, open and closed circles, covering all aspects of mediumship and psychic experience. In addition, two evenings each week are dedicated to healing which always has been an integral part of the College's life.

A 75th birthday is an important occasion and when it is a public body like the College of Parapsychology, a birthday celebration is very important. I hardly knew where to start. Celebrate we must but what to do and where to begin? Angela and I discussed how we should celebrate the event and we thought that a book would be a good way of commemorating it. I knew that we had some good archives and my Principal's drawer held a lot of 'stuff' which has never been seen outside of the College and I know that these are important pieces of our History.

We knew that our friend, Gerald O'Hara, had recently written a history of Spiritualism so we hoped that he and our good friend, Ann Harrison, who had helped with the editing and the publishing of his book, would be willing to work in creating something for the College. Both Gerald and Ann have given their time and effort as their contribution to our anniversary and I really thank them for it. What they have achieved is way in excess of what I had hoped and I am proud to be associated with the final result, "Mrs Miller's Gift". I never realised what a story lay behind the 75 years of the College's existence.

I believe, in the years to come, that the College will continue to play an important part in peoples' search for understanding whether it be of themselves or the work of Spirit. Mrs Miller was a woman of rare foresight and inner strength who left us a College as a legacy. When I came into the College, I discovered that it was dedicated to maintaining its independence for the sake of the people whom we serve. That was Mrs Miller's view and that is what her gift was dedicated to... a vision to serve other people. I know that other Principals before me have stayed true to that vision and I trust that the people, who take up the reins after I am gone, will maintain this ideal.

A College is a place of learning and, as Principal, I have learned that it is <u>the people</u> who make the College and I want to say to all those who have given of their time to work in the College, in whatever way - today or in the past, and also to those who have come in search of something, that, without you I could not have fulfilled my post, for there would be no College. To them and you all, I give my heartfelt thanks.

Let us go forward together serving others now so that in times to come they in their turn may be able to serve. We hope that you will enjoy this walk down memory lane and take pride in our great tradition and heritage. And when we meet by and by, let's have a dram and take counsel together.

Magnus McInnes

June 2007

Introduction

"And there's another country,
I've heard of long ago,
Most dear to them who love her,
Most great to them who know."

These lines from the famous hymn, 'I Vow to Thee my Country' nicely express the comfort to be found in a belief and emphasise the importance of knowledge. In one sense the hymn expresses the old conundrum: how do I know what I know? The Edinburgh Psychic College and Library sought to provide a faculty to establish, via study a new basis in experience for that knowing. "I experience, therefore I know", was the brief that underwrote and still underwrites the work of the College.

For to know something is to have learned about it, to have endeavoured to understand, to have explored the facets of that which we try to comprehend. In founding a Psychic College, the brief was fundamentally to provide facilities for individuals to explore, learn about and comprehend the psychic aspects of humanity. It sought also to provide comfort for the bereaved and assumed that the student was approaching the study and experience of the soul of man. It was, and still is, customary to speak of the 'after life'. Yet this 'after life' was experienced not as something altogether removed from this life, as if it was an abstraction 'a country of which we know little; on the contrary this 'other country' was one that was experienced as impinging itself on the consciousness as a daily reality.

Ethel Maud Miller, in founding the Psychic College and Library (now the Edinburgh College of Parapsychology) in September 1932, would have known that to many the pursuit of knowledge of that 'other country' was a religious quest for greater consciousness, leading to union with the divine. To a few, it was a form of worship, whereas to others Psychism or Spiritualism was the scientific study of anomalous phenomena. While some in a materialisation séance, where spirit became matter, found in materialisation that matter had become spiritualised and that they had encountered the living forces as emanations of God. For others it was a scientific anomaly. Many came to find succour for their heartache and consolation for their loss, while some came to satisfy their curiosity and to explore the unusual. Others came seeking an amusement. Ethel Miller took the brief that in providing facilities that were not tied to a religion, the enquirer could pursue as they wished the phenomena they sought.

The College was and still is, fundamentally, about providing a service. The purpose was to provide a relevant service that would be free of dogma or creed and would provide the seeker with the resources they needed. The objective was not to tie the seeker to a religious commitment. That brief was very relevant in 1932 and with foresight, generosity and wisdom, Mrs Miller's decision, laid down when founding the College, is still relevant today.

Once during World War II the College Principal, Mrs Catherine Allan, referred to the one-off service that the public sought. The College came to realise, that the point of entry the individual took in College facilities was sometimes where they stayed. The 'markets' were different for differing interests. The private sitter might not be a séance goer, or attend a lecture, large public demonstration, or development circle. Some did take up other activities and occasionally would go on to become the backbone of the College. The duty of the College was to provide an as-and-when service. If people wanted only one kind of service, e.g. a private sitting, then that is what the College was there to provide. The foregoing was as true in 1932, in 1943 and is true to this day.

The College's foundation came at a time when there was a "market" for such an establishment. The Spiritualist movement in the United Kingdom was at its zenith of popularity and influence. The period of the 1930's has been commented upon as being a "Golden Age" of Spiritualism. This period was a golden flowering of support and public interest.

However, this was not the only "Golden Age" that is claimed. The eight decades, from 1870's to 1951, each had their "signs and wonders" and produced some notable mediums. The first so called "Golden Age" of the 1870s, ending with the Dr Henry Slade trial in 1879, is thought by some to have brought about the decline of development and exhibition of physical mediumship but this did not happen. The Spiritualist Movement and the Edinburgh College were heirs to a strong tradition and process of development and I would propose a more comprehensive view of the "Golden Age" that would encompass the whole period from 1870 to 1951. With regard to the 1930s as a Golden era, essentially you cannot (as some try to) understand an era out of context. I would suggest that because a voice of the past is not heard does not mean that it did not speak beautifully and was influential in making the present what it has become.

I hope as an 'onlooker' to have been able to write an objective history of the College. I have not approached this work as a linear chronicle of events, as a journal of the years. I have linked each chapter to a theme and present the material according to its place in the scheme. The Edinburgh College is one of the few survivors from at least 20 Psychic Research societies of the 1930s. These narratives can be seen as an example for what may have occurred in other Colleges. The College's 75 years-rich experience can be seen as a snapshot of its age. In that way, I hope to present a story that becomes a contribution to Psychic and Spiritualist history.

However, the scheme in question does flow down through the years. The first chapter deals with the Millers and the influences that were an inspiration to Mrs Miller in founding the new College. In chapter two we examine the contribution of the 'names' within the Spiritualist movement whose involvement enhanced the rapid growth and expansion of the College and its activities. In chapter three physical mediumship is featured and I include material that has been rediscovered in the College's own library correcting the impression that Helen Duncan did not often serve the College. This chapter also has reports of the work of other mediums, including physical mediums, and speakers who served the College. The fourth chapter deals with transition and renewal of the College that occurred in the early 1970s and how the College found a new *raison de'être.*

My research for this book led to long hidden treasures in the recesses of the College building so I am delighed to be able to present a chapter, 'from the archives', as it were. The records, artefacts, memos, accounts, minute bookings, jottings, magazine clippings and ephemera that posterity has saved are the chance flotsam of a by-gone age that form the researcher's materials. The voices that have come down to us of those who were influential in shaping this story are those that fate has preserved. One would wish for other voices. How informative the journals of Mrs Miller or Miss Mowat would have been but these were never written.

Some attempt to put the archives into a coherent form was undertaken. However, the cataloguing long ago went awry and chaos now reigns. The voice that is most prominent in the records is that of the Principal and Treasurer, Robert Findlay whose notes and memos tell us of the transitional period of the 1970's. There are many other hand written notes and jottings, by an unknown author, written later in the 1970's and it is from these details that the main body of the book has been derived. One could wish for a more structured set of material but that which has been left to us is sufficient for the labour in hand and I pay my respects to the unknown author for the obvious work that went into saving something for the future. These narratives are further embellished by other voices. Mrs Allan has left us the speeches that she gave during the World WarII. Laura Culme-Seymour has left memorable accounts of her sittings in séances with Helen Duncan and others. Laura's book has given us a new understanding of the great medium's relationship with the College. Reports were gathered from newspapers both psychic and local, especially 'The Scotsman'. From such ephemera the story of the College emerges and is shaped.

This is the history of the College on its own terms. The phenomena that people say occurred is what they report and what they value. Many may take the view that the very idea of a Psychic College is ridiculous and therefore the 75 years of endeavour were wasted. We would reply - to the players of this book they were not a waste.

In a real sense the College itself is the hero of this book. For we are celebrating the 75th Anniversary with a biography of an institution. In the manner of biography, we have tried to present the people in terms that they themselves would have recognised. Where someone left an account of the value of their experience, we include it without comment. These voices of the College and its friends await you in the chapters to be read.

As L. P. Hartley said, *"The Past is a foreign country: they do things differently there."*

We have not attempted to include by name all the individual healers, mediums, librarians, cleaners, tea-ladies, drivers and 'welcomers' at the door, for, even if we could do so, the list of those who have served the College would fill another book. Unfortunately the records do not exist for this to happen so for those few whose names have been recorded in this book, keep in your memory all those who over the years have worked in the same capacity and whose names have not been recorded. They are not forgotten for it is for them and for you too that this book is written.

Our thanks go out to you all, past and present, for all your efforts to keep this College open for those who come to find what they need.

Gerald O'Hara.

Ethel Maud Miller

1 'I have a dream.........'

God finds Himself by creating..My beloved is ever in my heart
that is why I find him everywhere.

Rabindra Nath Tagore

Edinburgh is a very old city. It has many bad memories and a lot of good memories. Among the happier souvenirs for many people is the work done by the Edinburgh Psychic College and Library, now known as the Edinburgh College of Parapsychology. The foundation of the College came about on the 8th September1932 when a rich widow, Mrs Ethel Maud Miller (1876-1946), made the handsome donation of a fine Georgian house at 30 Heriot Row in the New Town.

It was a warren of a place, with a basement containing a sub-basement, kitchens, stone larders, vaults, wine cellars; servants' places and places the masters never went. The upper floors possessed an entry-hall, drawing rooms, a library, reception rooms, any number of bedrooms and disrobing rooms. The servants would attend to rooms with old privies, to bathrooms and fireplaces. The whole building was crowned with attics where the servants crowded together and slept. From out of the windows of the roof the views included the rocky spine that supports the castle of Edinburgh and the old town as it winds its way down to Holyrood. From the other side the vista took in the Firth of Forth towards Fife and on to the open sea. This teaming anthill of a structure was silent and for sale and then Mr Robert Ernest Miller died.

'Millionaires Row' is the nickname now given to the elegant row of terrace houses designed by Robert Reid in 1802-3. In early 2007, an apartment in Heriot Row (i.e. not the whole house), was to be had for rent for £3,250 pounds a month.

The new town, and in it later the new College, was situated in

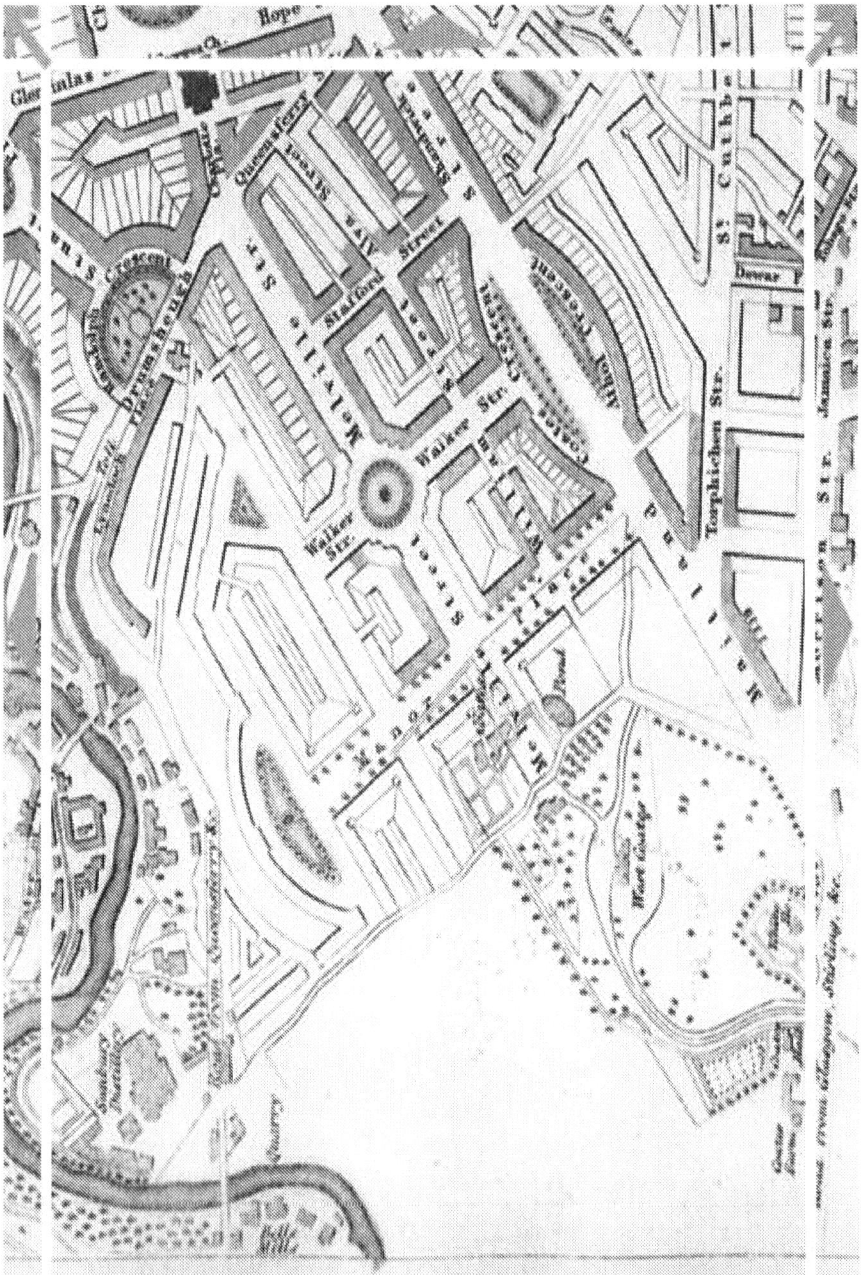

Edinburgh: showing part of the New Town with Melville Street in 1844.
(Heriot Row is just off the top of the page in this illustration)

Front elevation of a Robert Adams House in the New Town, late 18th Century.

a development to the north, beyond the stinking Nor Loch of old Edinburgh. James Craig had won the competition to build the New Town in 1766, by proposing a simple grid pattern on the classic Roman model. The first phase of development was completed by 1800 and the whole was finished by the 1830's. Many notable Scottish architects were involved with designs for the new town, including Colen Campbell, James Gibbs and Robert Adams. Their infusion of symmetry, proportion and strict sense of line were the outcome of the 'Grand Tour' through Europe and Italy. There they had picked up a language and aesthetic that we now think of as classical architecture. The architects of the New Town saw themselves as heirs to Roman virtues, such as civility, gravity and style. These principles they sought to elevate by the idiom of building. They produced books full of drawings and plans of classical orders and ornamentation which could be used by others and which served as an inspiration not only for builders but also for their clients. The expansion of the city matched the flowering of the Scots in the arts and sciences of the late 18th century, in what has become known as the Scottish Enlightenment.

Robert Ernest Miller

Robert Ernest Miller was a man of iron. The future Psychic College in "Millionaires Row" had been bought on the wages of iron. The sweat and labour of men had yielded up its profit in cold coin and white bank notes. Yet there is no evidence to suggest that the Miller family were heartless capitalists. Indeed the younger

Miller was a keen water colourist. Robert Ernest Miller and his twin brother, Thomas Frederick Miller, had been born on 8th of September 1873 in Canongate, Edinburgh. He was the second son, his brother Thomas Frederick being born fifteen minutes ahead of Robert and he was the third child of Thomas and Marion Miller (nee Brown). By the time of the census of 1881, the family was living at Norton Villa and had only one servant Mary Reid.

Thomas Miller, father of Robert Miller.

But the family prospered. Thomas Miller had established the iron foundry in 1867 and had later taken a partner, John Milne but in 1884 the partnership was dissolved. The firm of Miller and Co of the London Road Foundry had, according to one report, "become one of the most noted houses engaged in the iron industry not only in Edinburgh but in the whole of Scotland'.

Early 20th century illustration of the London Road Foundry

This report from the 'Edinburgh Illustrated' of the early 1900's goes on to state that Thomas Miller "originated the works" and their reputation had been built on the best "chilled rolls". This was a method of producing iron of any shape, for paper mill machinery, the railway industry and all forms of transport. Soon many industries were calling on Thomas Miller of London Road. The same report goes on to say that Thomas Miller had not had an easy time breaking in to the market and many stringent tests were required by the

The Foundry Yard

buyers of his goods. It was Miller's use of chilled iron that made him different from the steel manufacturers. Iron was thought of as 'old fashioned' in the age of the pliable strength of steel. Thomas Miller was running against the trend in production set by Sir Henry Bessemer (1813-98) who developed the Bessemer method of blowing air through the molten ore using the "Bessemer Converter". In an age of Iron and Steel it was not only the Millers who made fortunes. However, Thomas Miller's method of production was unique and 'There is no other iron foundry in Great Britain where the metallurgical operations are better conducted'. But it was the economic advantage of locally produced iron and its greater suitability to some forms of transport such as, tramways that eventually won Thomas Miller a lucrative market.

The rapid increase of the business necessitated frequent additions to the works. New drawing rooms for draughtsmen; general offices for administration and executive suites were required. The industry needed more furnaces and turning shops, which were added in quick succession. The whole site eventually covered three acres of Edinburgh. The siting of the Foundry was advantageous with good rail connections to the ports, and on to Europe and the Empire. A London office became a necessity and one was found at 16 Victoria Street, Westminster. Eventually agencies throughout the world were operating for Miller's London Road Iron Foundry.

Mrs Miller was half Norwegian; her mother's name being Brown and her father's being Hansen. That she was born in Norway is commonly said of her and no birth certificate can be found in this country's records. Ethel Maud Hansen had possibly met Robert Miller while he was on a trip to Norway and they are known to have visited the country frequently. They honeymooned in India. An account left to us by Mrs Miller's secretary, also Assistant Secretary to the College's Honorary Principal and Secretary, Catherine Mowat, describes Ethel Miller as being distraught at the death of her husband.

Frederick H. Myers (1843-1901)

Together, Ethel and Robert Miller had discussed and read literature on man's survival of death. Catherine Mowat noted that, the book by Frederick Myers' "Human Personality and its Survival of Bodily Death" (published posthumously in 1903) had been influential upon the couple's thinking. One of the subsequent visitors to the College was Geraldine Cummins whose automatic writing had produced the posthumous work said to be

Geraldine Cummings

by Frederick Myers, "Beyond Human Personality" and the "Road to Immortality". I wonder if Ethel Miller and Geraldine discussed the books? Certainly Ethel must have concluded on the lines of Revelations iv. that:-

"After this I looked, and behold, a door opened in heaven: and the first voice which I heard was as it were a trumpet talking with me; which said: Come up hither and I will show thee things, which must be hereafter. And I was immediately in the spirit."

After a while, in her home at Bonny Craig, Peebles, the rooms must have seemed very quiet. Ethel Miller (Ethel, meaning Noble in Old English) a wealthy woman, though always frail in health, was possessed of an indomitable spirit. Catherine Mowat speaks of her as being the "most generous and unselfish of people". That she was "unstinting" in support of the College and in her efforts to pass on the College free of debts after her death, is well known. By all accounts and there are now none alive who knew her, Mrs Ethel Maud Miller was "shy and retiring", "a gracious lady" and "unused to business". Mrs Miller sought out the solace to be found in the spirit contact provided to her by mediums. It was this solace that brought Mrs Miller to the realisation that everything that now mattered was in front of her eyes and, being familiar with the literature of Spiritualism, in buying and dedicating Heriot Row to Psychical Research many extraordinary things might be possible; like a trip to heaven, the possibilities of encountering her beloved Robert at a séance must have swum before her eyes? Ethel determined that the College would be dedicated to her husband in memoriam of their love, besides which, she and her beloved Robert had no child of their own.

The front elevation of Heriot Row looks over the south of Queen Street Gardens and if the authors of the built environment

No 30 Heriot Row was purchased by Mrs Miller in 1932 for the home of the Edinburgh Psychic College and Library

respected the balance and cultivation of the senses afforded by the new town, those that were the heirs to that estate have always honoured that vision. Melville Street, the second home of the newly renamed Edinburgh College of Parapsychology (1974), was designed by James Gillespie Graham and built between1822-30. Whether in Heriot Row, or later, in the College's new home in Melville Street the elegance of proportion and height of the rooms lent a grace to those who inhabited its halls.

As the Bible says, "In my Father's house there are many mansions". The widow decided that her fortune would be used to create such a mansion and that her new house would be dedicated to that Great Father's purpose. In short, 30 Heriot Row was a big house. There would be rooms enough to house the many spaces of the mind and to explore the psychic lives, the brotherhood and dimensions of Man.

Catherine Mowat tells us that the spirits urged the shy Ethel to found a College modelled on the British College of Psychic Science in London, which ran from 1920 to1939 but such was the "diffidence" of the lady that she was slow to act. There were Spiritualist churches in Edinburgh but there was none where an enquirer could go without commitment. James Hewat McKenzie and his wife had founded the British College of Psychic Science in London in 1920. The Edinburgh Psychic College and Library was closely modelled on the London College and Ethel Miller was greatly helped by the widow of James McKenzie, Barbara McKenzie who became a trustee of the new foundation. There were seven other colleges with the same aims as the Edinburgh College affiliated to the London College.

James Hewat McKenzie

Some of the story behind the founding of the London College is given in Leigh's "The Manual and Who's Who of British Spiritualism and Psychical Research for 1936". It is interesting to note that the Colleges are listed as Psychical Research Societies. At that time there were no such foundations as Independent Colleges. The London College, like its imitator in Edinburgh, was the outcome of the apparent need for a definite centre for the continuous and sustained study of mediumship. The emphasis being that the student could do so in an environment free of religious commitment. Further, the colleges aimed to minister to the wants of those who, interested in psychic possibilities, were inclined to make a serious study of them. James and Barbara McKenzie had been students of psychic phenomena since the early 1900's. Their first premises were in the west of London, at 59 Holland Park, W.11 and in 1929 they moved to 15, Queens Gate, SW7, Kensington,

In common with Edinburgh the financial risk of the venture fell on the shoulders of the founders. The London College became incorporated and at one time, Sir Arthur Conan Doyle (1859-1930) was its President. The Edinburgh College went down the route of becoming a Trust, Mrs B. Hewat McKenzie and Mr J. B. McIndoe, President of Spiritualist National Union (SNU) (1930-1938), being amongst the notables who assisted in the work. Along with many other alumni of the day, one person worth noting as showing an interest in the subject of survival is the eminent Swiss Psychiatrist, Dr Carl Gustav Jung who is listed as a Corresponding Member of the Society for Psychical Research (SPR) in London.

Both Colleges have, at some time, supported their own publication to promote their services and keep their students informed. The British College launched a quarterly in 1922 known as 'Psychic Science' but it wasn't until the late 1970s that Edinburgh had its own newsletter which was replaced by 'The Candlestick', in 1998 which is edited by the current College Secretary, George Cornick. The logo represents the principle that "the College does not claim to be that which shines forth light, but rather seeks to be a support for those that do so, giving light, wisdom, help and encouragement to seekers, whether from this side of life or the other."

There would be no Colleges if there were no mediums. The McKenzies, and the Edinburgh College would constantly seek out the best in the field of demonstrating mediums. Mrs Miller was keen also to provide the best environment for the workers. Meal times were to be set at a sufficient interval before the demonstration; no one was to be over worked and a fair remuneration was fixed in payment of services given. Retrospectively, the United Kingdom in the 1930s seems to have enjoyed a "Golden Age" of mediumship. It is worth noting, however, that in common with previous ages, the

A corner of the lounge, 30 Heriot Row from a press photograph of 1932

Psychic Press was constantly bemoaning the lack of good mediums. Accommodation was provided for visiting mediums, rooms for private consultations for clairvoyants and chambers for healing were also available.

A principle objective of the Colleges was to provide a full range of services to the enquiring student and to the public. Development classes were provided for those who wanted to practice and develop mediumship. A full programme of lectures was available and instruction and classes on many topics were provided. It was said to be Mrs Miller's dearest wish to found a great library as a research tool to the student, so much so that she insisted on the word library being incorporated in to the new college's title. The Edinburgh College still has a magnificent library, with some 3,000 volumes gracing its shelves. The desire for a great library was also shared by the McKenzies whose library in London was equally stacked with

PSYCHICAL RESEARCH SOCIETIES

EDINBURGH PSYCHIC COLLEGE AND LIBRARY

30, Heriot Row, Edinburgh, 3.
'Phone: No. 28193.

Weekly "At Homes," Wednesdays, at 3 p.m.; address and clairvoyance, followed by tea for those who so desire. Weekly Friday meetings, at 8 p.m. Lecture followed by demonstration of clairvoyance by medium in residence.

Affiliated to British College of Psychic Science, Ltd.

Hon. Principal and Secretary: Mrs. Ethel Miller, 30, Heriot Row, Edinburgh, 3.

Trustees: Mrs. Ethel Miller, 30, Heriot Row, Edinburgh, 3; Mrs. Hewat McKenzie (Hon. Principal, B.C.P.S., Ltd.), 1, Tudor Court, Hanworth, Middlesex; Mr. J. B. M'Indoe (President, S.N.U.), 157, Invergyle Drive, Cardonald, Glasgow, S.W. 2; Mr. W. Wilson (Solicitor), 43, Stevenson Street, Oban, Argyll.

Committee: Mrs. Hewat McKenzie (Advisory Member); Mr. J. B. M'Indoe (Advisory Member); Dr. D. McF. Barker, M.B., Ch.B. (Chairman of Committee); Mrs. L. MacDonald; Mrs. W. Roughead; Mrs. W. G. Scott; Mr. J. W. Herries; Mr. A. H. C. Lamb (W.S.).

Assistant Secretary: Miss C. Mowat.

Librarian: Miss J. Frazerhurst.

College founded by Mrs. Ethel Miller. Opened on September 8th, 1932. Dedicated by Rev. C. Drayton Thomas.

Materialisation Seances.—Mrs. Helen Duncan, of Edinburgh, will conduct group seances at the College once or twice per week whenever she is available. Members, 10s. 6d. Non-members, 12s. 6d.

Direct-Voice Seances.—It is hoped that arrangements can be made for Mrs. MacCallum, of Glasgow, to attend the College once per month during this session.

Group Sittings.—Group sittings are held with visiting mediums on Tuesday evenings at 8 p.m., and Thursday afternoons at 3 p.m. Bookings must be made in advance.

Library.—The library contains over 750 books on psychic subjects, and is being steadily added to. Catalogues, 6d. each. New supplement can be obtained separately. Price 2d. each. A deposit may be left for postage by members wishing books to be forwarded to them.

Subscription Fees.—Members, £1 1s. per annum; Associate members, 10s. 6d. per annum.

Members have free entrance to all regular meetings, use of library and reduced fees for demonstrations. Associate members

Edinburgh College's entry in the 'Manual and Who's Who of Spiritualism and Psychical Research for 1936'.

many volumes and we may assume that Mrs Miller also took up other aspects of James McKenzie's regime in London and the same high standards would be expected of the mediums visiting Edinburgh.

The 1930s was the age of some well-known physical mediums. As shown in the College's entry in the 1936 'Manual & Who's who' (see *p.29*), the well-known physical medium Helen Duncan would travel from her address at Wauchope Place in Craigmillar, Edinburgh to the College to give séances, as did a Mrs MacCallum, a direct voice medium of Glasgow. There are records of the work of this medium too and these are included in this book. Before the College was established the psychic photographer, William Hope, whose photograph is shown on page 38 with one of his psychic photographs, also travelled to Edinburgh to give photographic sittings.

The standards of the College were set very high and this was reflected in the environment provided for the workers. Many great names of the day served the College but it is worth remembering that to the individual studying mediumship or the sitter looking for evidence the true value of personal experience can rarely be estimated.

Eileen Garrett in her autobiography, "My Life" (1939) wrote of James H. McKenzie, as, " a most remarkable personality and his humorous outlook and generous welcome, made me want to know him better, I dined with him and realised that he had a greater knowledge and understanding of psychic phenomena, than anyone I had yet met". Garrett undertook to train under the supervision of James Hewat McKenzie and receive a retainer while she did so. Eileen Garrett continues, "(His) lofty conception

Eileen Garrett. Her autobiography gives an insight to the work of the Edinburgh College.

of mediumship was something I had not come across before. He emphasised the responsibility which possessing this power placed upon me. He emphasised leading a quiet and harmonious life, free from excess of alcohol, sex and elaborate food. My whole responsibility lay in living this simple and controlled existence". There were aspects of severity that seem unlikely, given the character of Ethel Miller, to have been put into practice at Edinburgh. Submission to all instructions was required and Eileen Garrett continues she had to "obey rigid disciplines...in order to keep my mediumship free of sub-conscious influence".

Barbara McKenzie

The McKenzies and Mrs Miller were good friends and Ethel found much in the couple to inspire her in the founding of the Edinburgh College. Garrett says of the McKenzies, "I had come to value and trust the integrity of understanding, which both he and his wife possessed". I feel that this trust, integrity and understanding must also have impressed itself on Mrs Miller, who was greatly influenced by them. Barbara McKenzie and her colleague, Rose Champion de Crespigny, Principal of the British College, who died in 1937, became close friends of Mrs Miller and both ladies presided over many events at the new College in Edinburgh.

Both McKenzies were Scots. Barbara McKenzie being born in the North of Scotland(1) of Presbyterian and Labour Party background. Born in 1870 she left Scotland to become a teacher in London where she met and married James in 1895. He came from a background that was "almost Calvinistic in its harsh discipline". He left school at thirteen to join his father's ironmongery and tool making business.

He was said to be driven by a need to self-improve and "read avidly" of the classics. He left home to escape the tyranny of his father and went to London where he met his future wife. Logie Barrow in his landmark book, "Independent Spirits" supports the view that Spiritualism attracted people who were independent of mind, that tolerated a democratic model of participation and who were therefore inclined to support socially progressive causes. My own book "Dead Men's Embers" shows that a local Spiritualist society (York) did support a wide variety of socially progressive causes. Keir Hardie, the future Labour leader, from Lanark was known to have attended séances.

The Edinburgh College was heir to a now partly forgotten tradition. The Edinburgh College was seeking to empower the enquirer or student, not to enrol them in to a commitment to a religious viewpoint. David Richmond(2) the First 'Missionary' Spiritualist medium in 1853 was self-taught, self-employed, said that "On our arrival at Glasgow we dropped some seed corn and at Edinburgh."(3) by which he meant that he had preached Shakerism and Spiritualism. This may be the earliest reference to Spiritualism in Edinburgh.

The independent and non-committed view of Spiritualism that the Edinburgh College was to follow found its most articulate exponent in another Scotsman, James Burns (1835-1894). Born in Ayrshire he had, as the editor of the magazine, 'The Medium and Day Break', opposed all attempts at national organisation of Spiritualists. He was typically a man of the 19th century whose view of Spiritualism was one of radical egalitarianism. It was a view taken by many and remains in evidence to this day. Like the McKenzies he was said to "have had a great aptitude for learning and spent all his time and money on pursuits of a progressive nature". He opposed all attempts at Spiritualist organisation because he thought it would lead to hierarchy, priest-craft and dogma. Burns was excited by the non-Christian possibilities of Spiritualism. His socially progressive attitudes were mirrored in the many campaigns he and other Spiritualists supported. Whereas we may now take independence of mind for granted, it was not so in the 19th and early 20th century.

An author known as Fritz[4] wrote one of the clearest statements of the independence of mind required to support so highly unpopular a cause such as Spiritualism.

"...a man must, therefore be independent, or by reason of his poverty or by reason of his wealth, before he can defy the opinion of the World"

Social conformity was much greater in the period under study than now and the need to conform may well have been determined by one's financial standing. Spiritualism was reviled and its supporters persecuted and prosecuted. Spiritualism, through its practices could transcend the class barriers and also empower women to a role outside of the home. In this look at background influences 'Fritz's' comment as to wealth, independence or poverty being a precondition to supporting Spiritualism, seems to me as good a definition of the nature of Spiritualist support as any and one which was upheld by what we know of the Edinburgh College. Spiritualist support emerges from the self-employed, the working-man or artisan or from those of independent means, such as Ethel Miller. This broader view of the class nature of support is borne out in 'Dead Men's Embers'.[5]

Through these snippets and through her associations with others and further, via inference, as to the nature of the movement which Mrs Ethel Miller was prepared to financially underwrite, we can obtain a fuller picture of the lady. We know already that she was wealthy, slightly built, always frail in health but possessed of an indomitable spirit; that she was the most generous and unselfish of people and unstinting in her support of the College. Gracious and unassuming, Ethel, with her voice, low-toned and gentle, was unused to business. Shy and retiring as she was, she was still prepared to seek spirit contact, provided to her by mediums, though such contact was disapproved of socially. Undoubtedly, she was a person of trust and integrity who was concerned that her institution should match the high standards, both in education and mediumship of the College in London. Clearly Mrs Miller wanted to provide the best accommodation and provision possible to her workers, more than likely without the strictness of the regime found at the London College. By inference, Ethel Miller was prepared to meet her social inferiors on terms of civility. Obviously, Ethel must have been a person who was herself a worker and one prepared to take advice and help from more knowledgeable friends; someone prepared to help organise and engage the voluntary efforts of others, so that many were permitted to preside over meetings at the College. It is clearly evident that authority without responsibility was not part of Mrs Miller's make-up but the shy Mrs Miller did not, through patronage, seek presidency over her new institution.

The launch of the College came at a time, in the 1930s, which saw Spiritualism's greatest flowering. There is today speculation among historians as to the extent of support for Spiritualism in the 1930s but Jenny Hazelgrove[6] states that in 1914 there were 145 churches affiliated to the SNU and 500 was the number declared by Maurice Barbanell in Psychic News in 1932.

John Brown McIndoe, President of the SNU 1930-38

From the lists given in 'The Manual and Who's Who of Spiritualism and Psychical Research for 1936', 527 churches and Temples were affiliated to the SNU (not including Barbados). Thirty independent churches are listed but the exact number of independent churches and societies can only be guessed at. Also there were 14 Psychical Research Societies (which includes Edinburgh Psychic College and Library) and 16 large Independent Societies are mentioned.

Efforts to assess the strength of the Greater World Christian Spiritualist League at this time are hazardous. However, 'The Manual for 1936'[7] says "Already to date (September 1935) 580 Churches are affiliated to the League". It also mentions that there were 20,000 individual members in this country and overseas.

In Edinburgh only 2 societies are listed as affiliated to the SNU; Edinburgh Association of Spiritualists at 9, Gayfield Square and Edinburgh - Scottish Psychologian Society: 22, Stratford Street but there may have been other independent societies and churches.

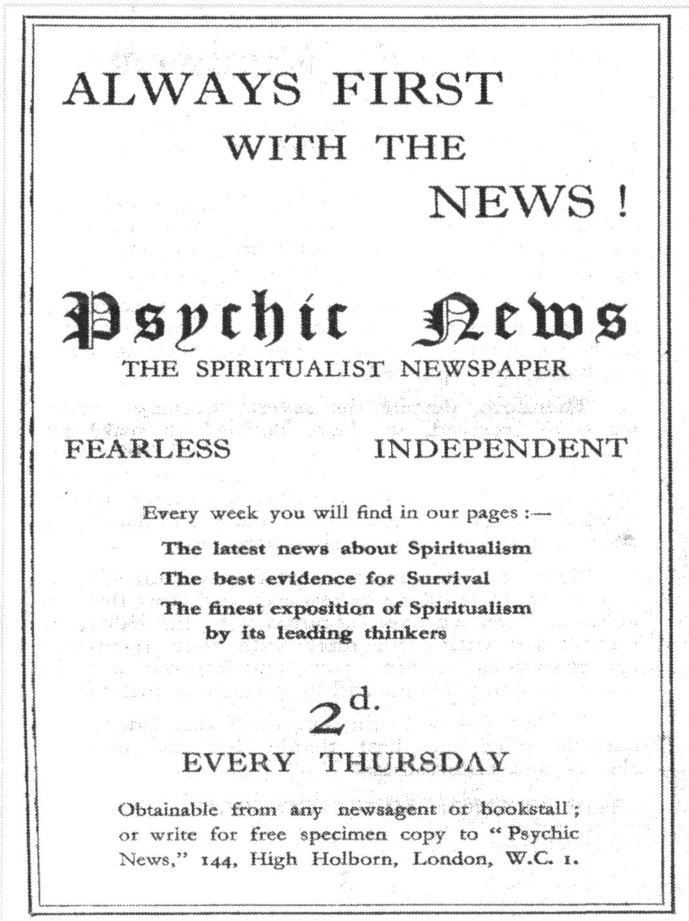

An advertisement for Psychic News founded by Maurice Barbanell and Jack Rubens with financial help from Arthur Findlay in 1932, just prior to the foundation of the Edinburgh College

The nature of support for the Spiritualist movement fell into different categories; there was the church member, the enquirer (or the curious), the researcher, the student, the bereaved and the séance goer, some of whom did not go to any other event. One form of tacit support, that Jenny Hazelgrove(8) does mention, is the large public meeting. These were a common feature of the day and many were held on all manner of topics. Hannen Swaffer with Helen Hughes held large meetings at the Usher Hall up to the Second World War. These public meetings were very popular, both in London and around the United Kingdom. The medium, Helen Hughes, regularly addressed crowds of 3,000. While Estelle Roberts addressed 9,000 at the Royal Albert Hall. 'Names' could be made on the circuits of national halls. These events could be thought of as analogous to the T.V. mediums of today such as Colin Fry and Tony Stockwell. These modern mediums draw packed houses at theatres around the country whose audiences can be thought of as the 'fellow travellers' of Spiritualism.

The world of 1932 was a difficult environment in which to launch a new venture and we have seen that Ethel Miller was prepared to underwrite the costs and to indemnify, the College from financial ruin as far as possible. Following the Wall Street crash of October 1929, Britain had seen unemployment rise to 2,700,000 which in effect meant that 7 million were reliant on the meagre dole. Winston Churchill had been obliged to take the pound off the Gold Standard by which the currency was underwritten.

A lively Spiritualist scene in the U.K. makes up the background to the foundation of the Edinburgh College. Sir Arthur Conan Doyle had died in 1930[9] with a memorial meeting being held in the Royal Albert Hall, which was addressed by the great and the good of Spiritualism. In May of 1931, Winifred Moyes had founded the Greater World Christian Spiritualist League, having first been entranced by her spirit guide Zodiac in 1920. Also in 1932, Arthur Findlay helped financially to found Psychic News, with and under the editorship of Maurice Barbanell[10], to be the Independent Voice of the whole Spiritualist movement. The book, "On the Edge of The Etheric", by Arthur Findlay became the Spiritualist publishing sensation of the decade, being reprinted 25 times between November 1931 and June 1932 and it has subsequently been translated in to19 languages.

Also in 1932 Geraldine Cummins' "The Road to Immortality" was published, which by 1967 had four editions and had been translated into many tongues.

On the Edge of the Etheric

OR

Survival after Death Scientifically Explained

BY

J. ARTHUR FINDLAY

With the Preface to
An Investigation of Psychic Phenomena
BY THE LATE
SIR WILLIAM BARRETT, F.R.S.
Professor of Physics, Royal College of Science for Ireland from 1873 to 1910
Past President, London Society for Psychical Research

Published for the Author by
RIDER & CO.
PATERNOSTER ROW
LONDON

J.Arthur Findlay, Author of 'On the Edge of the Etheric', 'Rock of Truth' and a number of other books and Honorary Member of the Edinburgh Psychic College.

In 1932,with the United Kingdom under the Scots born Prime Minister Ramsey MacDonald, hunger riots occurred in Britain; Charles Lindbergh's baby was found dead after he had paid a fortune in ransom; the month of May, saw Amelia Earhart fly the Atlantic and Aldous Huxley published 'Brave New World'... "that has such people in it"...... In October, Oswald Mosley launched the British Union of Fascists under the Lightning flash emblem, (derided by its critics as a flash in the pan). In November, Franklin Delano Roosevelt won a landslide victory in the U.S. Presidential elections on the "New deal" slogan. By the close of the year, Hitler's Nazi party became the biggest in the Reichstag and in India the British banned Mahatma Gandhi's Congress Party and threw him into jail, whilst at the cinema you could have seen James Cagney in "Scarface" and, on Christmas Day, King George V made the first ever Christmas broadcast from Sandringham in Norfolk.

In March the following year the much loved psychic photographer William (Billy) Hope died and was buried in Manchester whilst in Edinburgh, in May, Helen Duncan faced trial for the first time.

William 'Billy' Hope with one of his photographs. Although he died only six months after the College opened, many originals of his work have been found in the College archive.

A group photograph taken at Crewe with one of the many clerics of the period who were associated with Spiritualism.

But for us more significantly, on Wednesday 8th of September 1932 the doors of the Edinburgh Psychic College and Library were formally opened. The college had been furnished from out of Mrs Miller's own money. She had contributed watercolours that her husband had executed and also a fine portrait of Thomas Miller, which still hangs in the College. From notes used as the basis for the college leaflet we learn that Mrs Miller intended the College to be a memorial to her late husband. There is also an aside as to Mrs Miller's religious opinions, which was not subsequently used in the leaflet, "Mrs Miller's great desire was that mediumship should be regarded as a divine gift and all possessing it should be given every facility for its expression under the best conditions." This is the only reference found as to Mrs Miller's personal opinion on religious matters.

A leaflet printed for the Golden Jubilee in 1982 is also the source of Catherine Mowat's memories of Mrs Miller. The original handwritten history also tells us that the College absorbed an earlier organisation to wit: - The Scottish Psychic Society (S.P.S). In the manner of any sound business venture it must be assumed that Mrs Miller took counsel on the "market" for the proposed new College. Contacts must have been sought out and some contacts must have been pre-existing. A nucleus of supporters would have come in to assist with establishing the College as a project. A core membership from the S.P.S. may have been absorbed. The earliest extant membership figure available is from November 1937 and records 240 members. In 1937 Mrs Miller took her last trip to her native Norway and is reported to have been in poor health from 1938. Sometime thereafter she left her Peebles home and moved into the College. In the same year Ethel gave up her posts and became Chairman of Trustees. Mrs Catherine Allan took over the administration, holding the post of Honorary Principal until1960 when she was well in her eighties.

Networking, as we would call it these days, must have helped the "shy and retiring" Ethel to launch the College. The well known London based Spiritualist, the Reverend Charles Drayton Thomas formally opened the College and "paid eloquent tribute to those responsible". He referred to a message he had received from the late

Dr Lamond,[11] who was quoted, by Drayton Thomas,[12] as saying of the post-mortem world "I feel like a laddie on a new adventure".

Rev. C. Drayton Thomas

Rev. Dr. J. Lamond as the sitter in a photograph taken by Billy Hope at Crewe.

The bulk of his address was on the topic of "Unseen Powers at Work". The other speaker that night was Scotsman, John Brown McIndoe, President of the S.N.U between 1930-1938. He became a Trustee and Committee member of the new College, taking an active part in the life of this new venture.

Drayton Thomas concluded his address by saying:-

"It was natural for men and women of goodwill, when some great and good thing had been given to them, to wish that others might enter into the same light of love and joy. And they wanted it known that these beautiful premises had been secured and had been dedicated to this special work".

2 'Consider yourself one of the family .....'

"As you know, I don't believe in talking down to children, you are capable of grasping more than is generally appreciated by your elders. Education is a leading out, from e, out and duco, I lead."
'The Prime of Miss Jean Brodie'

Catherine Allan was an able and well-liked Honorary Principal of the Edinburgh College for 23 years. She died in 1966 aged 94. Mrs Allan had retired as Principal in 1960 and had been succeeded by Mrs Simpson. Catherine Allan was said by her friend, Maurice Barbanell, the editor of Psychic News, to have filled the post of Principal "...with distinction, grace and charm for 23 years". Barbanell continues, that she had no intention of staying on this earth for 94 years and having survived one serious operation Mrs Allan herself had said to the editor "I was so near the other side, but they sent me back. I will never die. I will have to be shot."

Mrs Catherine Allan

As so often with those who lead and are admired for their contribution to the Spiritualist movement, Catherine Allan had come to the role of Principal reluctantly. The lady herself said, "...it was the last thing that I wanted." In a sense the role chose her. Upon being told that her youngest son George had been killed in a motor cycling accident in Surrey, Mrs Allan is quoted as saying, "I can see myself, I was frozen." Life went blank for her. It was her sister-in-law, said to be "orthodox" in matters of religion, who said to Catherine "...you can't go on like this, you are breaking your heart." Upon making enquiries and being told of Spiritualism, Catherine replied, "What's that?" Already in her 60's, Mrs Allan agreed to go with her sister-in-law to a meeting at the Edinburgh Association of Spritualists' home at Gayfield Square in Edinburgh. The "un-professional" medium was a Mrs Bisset who told Catherine that "she would in three months, weeks or days have something come into her life that bring her ultimate happiness." The lady herself thought this quite impossible.

In the phrasing of the 19th century Catherine Allan's sister-in-law had become sufficiently "untrammelled by orthodoxy" as to propose that the two of them go to a séance with Helen Victoria Duncan. Their first sitting "was very crowded" and Mrs Allan could not see very much and was not very impressed. However, shortly after that they went to another sitting with only ten people present. There she received a spirit message which she says "suddenly broke the gloom that was over me." Mrs Duncan's "control" Albert, gave his first message that evening to Mrs Allan. Her son materialised and amongst other things said that he had heard his father and brother Rex saying that they regretted having no photograph of him. The materialised form of her son said, "If you go into my case you will find a wallet there. There are two photographs in it. I like the one on my motorcycle best". Catherine Allan tells us, "Rex said he would go up stairs and discover if it were true. He found his brother's case and within it the wallet. On examination he found the two snapshots as described in the message."

Helen Duncan

Mrs Helen Hughes of Seaham Harbour, County Durham, the

well-known clairvoyant medium who knew Catherine Allan well, also gave the future College Principal a message at a Gayfield Square meeting. Helen Hughes told Mrs Allan "...she was going to do a great work for Spiritualism. "Such was the retiring nature of Mrs Allan that she thought, "I could not see how this could come true." Helen told her that she would become Principal of the College and so it came about. Mrs Allan agreed to deputise for Mrs Miller when that lady went on a trip to Norway in 1937. Mrs Miller, whom we have noted as being of indifferent health never took up the reins again and Mrs Allan continued in the role of Principal until ill heath and old age forced her to retire in 1960.

J.W. Herries, who knew Mrs Allan well, this time in 1952, says of her, "she exercised a wise discretion, never obtrusive but always an important influence in the background:" The pleasant atmosphere of the college was also attributed to "careful and friendly supervision" such harmony and welcome are not easily maintained and such was said to be noticeable to the public. The visiting speakers also frequently commented on the fine ambience of the Edinburgh College saying that "...this greatly helped their effectiveness both on the public platform and in the private séance." In addition to the above Mrs Allan possessed good business acumen and a sound knowledge of administration.

Maurice Barbanell,
Founder and Editor of Psychic News

Maurice Barbanell also spoke of Catherine Allan as having a radiant personality and as being mentally alert up to the time of her death at 94. The editor, who knew her well and often chaired or spoke at meetings at the College concluded, "She was always to be seen at her desk on the ground-floor room where visitors were greeted with a beaming smile. Catherine was the perfect hostess to all Speakers and for those Speakers who were accommodated on the premises she regarded nothing as being too much trouble to make them comfortable". With her own death in view she had this to say, "I am looking forward to the happiness of joining my relatives and friends in the world beyond".

This simple statement of faith underlines much of the work done then and still being done by the Edinburgh College of Parapsychology. For while the College is committed to no dogma or creed and it has always aimed to give the enquirer an impartial evaluation of survival evidence, nevertheless, those who lead did then and still do have a spiritual nature that occasionally finds expression. Mrs Allan during the Second World War would often conclude her annual speech to the AGM. with a simple statement that all could agree with. At the AGM. of 1939/40 Mrs Allan said:

"It is up to us in Edinburgh who have not yet felt the full dastardly nature of this war to do all we can to keep this building as an oasis of Light in a desert of darkness and horror." In 1941 Catherine Allan added this to her annual address, "The ever-increasing number who earnestly seek information regarding psychic studies is evidence of the vital need that a centre such as ours supplies to the community, both spiritually and intellectually and inspires us to go forward with fresh heart knowing that we are helping to build a lasting peace out of the present chaos." In November 1944 looking forward to the year ahead, which surely would bring about a peace, Catherine Allan had this to say about the future "It is my earnest prayer that the coming year, may bring with it Peace, a real and lasting one, not simply a laying down of arms".

Catherine Allan's title was Honorary Principal of the college. A College is by definition an institution of education and is usually associated with a higher institution of learning in the manner of a college in a University. The Edinburgh Psychic College and Library was in association with sixteen other such Colleges, headed by the British College in London. In latter years the College has been in Kindred Body status to the Spiritualist National Union. The founders of the College set the agenda for the new institution to provide anopportunity to the curious to learn of the psychic side of Man.

An unknown author in1979 has left for posterity copious hand-written notes on the work of the College from its earliest beginnings up to the end of the 1970's. These notes are in no particular order and the handwriting is difficult to read. Yet these notes remain informative and as a researcher, one would dearly like to have known from where the information was collected. The author offers the following insight to the public lectures given at the College and occasionally elsewhere by leading speakers. The list is a long one with 21 subjects being listed between June 1933 and July 1937. The first recorded public lecture was given at the College on the subject of: -"Obsession---domination by Spirit?" Other topics covered that year included "Psychic phenomena - the main purpose for which the College started". Notable journalist and Spiritualist, Hannen Swaffer, spoke in October 1933 on the subject "Spiritualism and the New World"; one wonders which World Mr Swaffer had in mind when he proposed that topic.

Hannen Swaffer speaking at Durham Miners' Gala 1935

The College was to take a leading role in Edinburgh, in taking Spiritualist topics out to the populace at large. Large public meetings were a general feature of the age and were to continue in popularity until the advent of television more or less made public speaking and debate redundant. "Public meetings" were given by many groups in society and were opportunities to see national figures in various fields speaking in public. One public meeting given in Edinburgh's

Music Hall, in March 1934 under the sponsorship of the College had Maurice Barbanell and Hannen Swaffer speaking at what was called a "Propaganda Meeting".

Helen Hughes was a frequent contributor to the lecture platform of the College speaking for the first time in March 1934 on the topic of "Psychic Experiences". In May of the same year at the Central Hall, Tollcross, an unknown speaker spoke in trance on the subject of "Power" to an audience of one thousand people. In September of 1935, the editor of 'Two Worlds' gave an address at the College on "Personal Experience of the Trance State". This was followed by demonstration of Transfiguration but the medium's name is not given.

There is no reason to suppose that the meetings ceased after 1937 given the popularity of such meetings and the evidence of the ticket shown below. These occasions would also be held at some profit to the Psychic College and Library. However, the records are patchy and there are no further records until after the outbreak of the Second World War.

EDINBURGH PSYCHIC COLLEGE
30 HERIOT ROW

PROPAGANDA MEETING

In the USHER HALL

On FRIDAY, 24th SEPTEMBER 1943

At 7.30 p.m. Doors open 6.45

RESERVED, 2s. 6d.

Ticket for the 1943 Propaganda Meeting found in the archive at the College. Propaganda meetings were used to raise awareness of the fight for repeal of the Witchcraft Act under which Helen Duncan was charged.

Catherine Allan in her speeches for the early part of the War often mentioned that they had to work in reduced and difficult circumstances (presumably of blackout and travel restrictions). However, the random notes left by our unknown chronicler, lists several such successful public war-time meetings at the Usher Hall and elsewhere. The first was on the 24th September 1943 when Maurice Barbanell was speaking and Helen Hughes giving the demonstration with Mrs Miller and Catherine Allan in attendance.

It is not clear for whom our scribe was writing but it appears that they may have been compiling notes for a history and that the notes were written years later than the event is evident from the fact that the notes were in ballpoint, which was not invented until after 1945, (by the Hungarian, Mr Biro) and the pages also contain occasional literary comments. The following is the comment on the Usher Hall meeting of '43, speaking of Hughes and Barbanell.

"These outstanding figures in the fraternal work of the Spiritualist movement, have shared their gifts ... have brought enlightenment, comfort, and inspiration to many people restoring courage and hope to bereaved people".

The College held these large public meetings as anniversary commemorations. At one such meeting, in 1944, Helen Hughes was said to have delivered thirty to forty messages to the audience. The

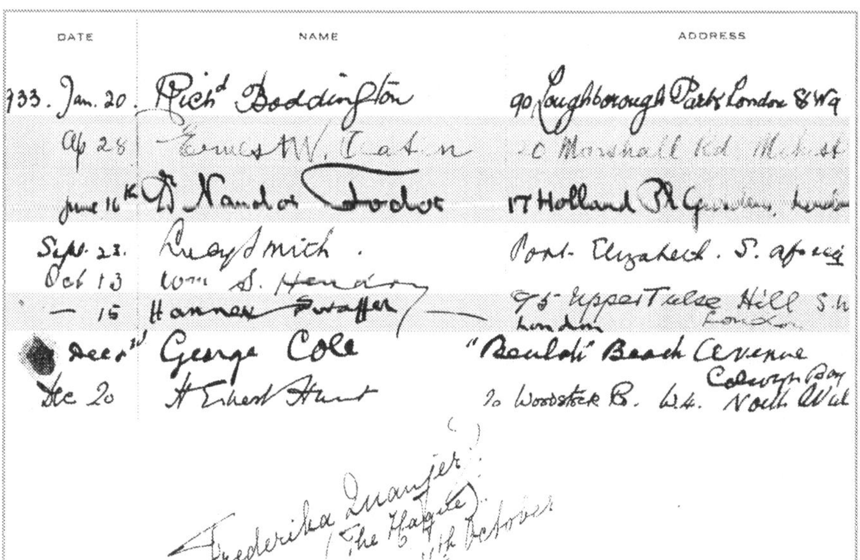

First page from the Visitors' Book of the Edinburgh Psychic College, 1933. Note the signatures of Ernest Oaten, Dr. Nandor Fodor, Hannen Swaffer and the author Richard Boddington.

Duchess of Hamilton was also noted as the speaker at the meeting. (A generation before, the Duchess of Caithness had been a prominent aristocratic supporter of Spiritualism).

The record is a useful insight into many aspects of the life of the College but that they are not a complete record of activities is obvious from the omission of the mention of a meeting which was addressed by Hannen Swafffer.

The Usher Hall was booked for another meeting in 1947, which was again addressed by Barbanell and Hughes and in 1948 the famous healer Harry Edwards gave a triumphant demonstration of his gifts. A report from 'The Sunday Post' says "about 2000 people of all ages packed the Usher Hall, Edinburgh last night and saw 17-year old Jessie Devine walk for the first time in her life. Harry Edwards of London, at a healing service organised by the Edinburgh Psychic College had just treated Jessie. Jessie came on to the stage supported by two friends. The huge audience hushed as she told him that she had suffered from spinal curvature. "She had never been able to walk". The lengthy report concluded with this. "This has made me very happy. Now I am going to be a nurse to help people crippled as I was". Another recipient of healing was quoted as saying "Oh I am so happy," she cried, "it's gone." After several other "miraculous" healings, 'The Sunday Post' report concludes, "When the service ended there were still scores of people lined up hoping to be cured of their complaints".

Harry Edwards, Healer extraordinaire

The following year, 1949 for no given reason the venue was switched to the New Cavendish Hall. Large public meetings organised by the College were to continue at the Usher Hall and elsewhere well into the late 1960s.

There is reason to think that a change of style may have seemed appropriate i.e. a "Brains Trust". This new form of radio debate, was copied from the BBC, now to be applied to all things psychic. The televised form is now taken for granted but originally it was developed for the radio where a knowledgeable panel of experts

A Psychic Brains Trust

Under the auspices of Edinburgh Psychic College a brains trust was held at 30 Heriot Row last night. The platform party consisted of the Rev. W. B. Taverner, Mr Maurice Barbanell, Mr J. W. Herries (questionmaster), Prof. K. W. Braid, Mrs Helen Hughes, and Mr Cecil Chapman. (" *News* " *photo.*)

The first Psychic Brains Trust at Edinburgh Psychic College 1952

from different fields would take questions from the public on important issues of the day.

On the 14th of September 1952, Helen Hughes, Maurice Barbanell and other friends, namely, the Rev. Taverner, Professor Braid and Mr Chapman (a research chemist of Glasgow) formed the panel and Mr J.W. Herries, acted as chairman for the meeting, which was held at Heriot Row.

The format was a success and the following year the meeting was held at the larger venue of the New Cavendish Ballrooms, Tollcross. The same "panel" was present and the questions ranged from questions of survival, scripture, whether or not the old testament prophets could communicate today (answer: yes, though the ancients prefer anonymity) and finally, "weren't spirit messages really rather trivial?" The reply was that the discourses received in home circles were extremely deep in philosophical content.

In summary, education, psychic service and exploration of the mind were the overriding brief of the new college. The directors of the new establishment were innovative and outgoing in their approach to carrying out their duties. And the college certainly attracted many prominent figures from several fields that were interested in the psychic nature of Man.

James William Herries (1875-1960) was a good friend to the College and through his pen and influence, an important benefactor. He had, since 1916, been Chief reporter for Scotland's leading newspaper, 'The Scotsman'. Herries retired from the paper in 1946 and died in November 1960. He was a close friend of Catherine Allan and undoubtedly was close also to Mrs Miller.

J.W. Herries

James Herries was born at Maxwelltown, Kirkcudbrightshire and joined the Dumfries Standard in 1895. He came from an affluent family which was connected to Sir James Barrie the playwright. He is quoted in his obituary as being one of the founders of the Psychic College. Without doubt, he was a talented man with interests, in painting, writing plays and poetry, working in stained glass. It is to this gentleman's acumen as a reporter that the "Loch Ness Monster " came to the modern world's attention. Noticing some local reports tucked away at the bottom of a page, Herries, commissioned a report that soon spread all over the pages of the World. He witnessed the surrender of the German fleet in 1918 and as a reporter attended the Peace conference at Versailles in 1919. He said at his retirement in1946 that his life "had been a front seat at the pageant of life." Among his many achievements were a number of plays, which went into production. In addition he was an able public speaker and spoke on Spiritualism and other topics over 270 times in Scotland during World War II. He was attracted to Journalism because of its crusading possibilities and in politics he never swerved from Liberalism.

In common with Lord Northcliffe (the publishing magnate), whom Hannen Swaffer greatly respected, Herries was also known as 'The Chief'. His pen was often dedicated to the service of the Psychic College and Library with many reports being written and published by James W. Herries. His influence was so great that whereas the new set-up without him would have had to struggle for coverage in the Press, with him as chief reporter to the College a wealth of invaluable publicity was guaranteed. It is through Herries that most of the early reports of the College's activities were written. What exactly his role as "founder member" was cannot now be established but he was certainly influential in promoting the College and his many reports filled the pages of 'The Scotsman' and by extension, those other newspapers that were syndicated to it. He was a keen ghost hunter and we shall come back to this aspect of psychic enquiry later. He chaired numerous meetings for and at the College and was a member of the council and a Trustee. Herries wrote a book on Direct Voice communications with the Misses Moore, entitled "Other World People" and in his book "I came, I saw" he gives us, as he says, some of the 'spice of life' in a series of articles from his life, including one on R.L. Stevenson's interest in Psychic Research. On the day Herries died he was performing conjuring tricks for his grandchildren. He was apt to finish an article in the press with the phrase "end story" but to this talented and much loved man, in his end was his beginning.

Herries certainly knew Hannen Swaffer (1879-1962)who was born in Lindfield, Sussex and educated at Stroud Green, Grammar School in Kent. He became a prominent drama critic and was well known for his sharp pen which caused him to be banned from various theatres. He latterly boasted that he was banned from forty-one auditoriums. He was a lifelong Socialist and in the 1930s a frequent speaker at the Durham miners Gala. Up to 1957 he was a member of the Labour Party. He argued, as did many that

Spiritualism and Socialism were two halves of a great whole. His "Chief" Lord Northcliffe nicknamed Swaffer, "the Poet" as Hannen affected a Bohemian style of dress that involved a black-frock coat and black cravat suitable to a drama critic.

'The Bohemian' Hannen Swaffer

He is more commonly remembered as the "the Pope of Fleet Street" not because he became an avowed Spiritualist but because his style of writing could sometimes, when he was roused to anger, be rather pontificating. However, he is highly readable.

He is credited with turning the Daily Mirror, from a failing womens' newspaper into a mass circulation daily. He espoused many causes and after the death of his chief, 'Swaff', (as Tom Driburg, his biographer, and others referred to him) became a Spiritualist through the fine mediumship of Mrs Osborne Leonard.

He tells us in his book "Northcliffe's Return" that his first posthumous encounter with his old boss came in South Norwood, London with a young trance medium by the name of Potter. He had come into contact with Dennis Bradley who invited him to attend séances at his home in Barnes, West London. It was there in the 'Direct Voice' that he again spoke to his old mentor and chief.

"Northcliffe's Return" became an immensely popular book. It was translated into several languages and through Northcliffe's worldwide network of publications the book was syndicated throughout the globe.

Swaffer became a regular visitor to the Edinburgh College and addressed many meetings both there and in the large halls of the Scottish capital. He was a fiery and impassioned speaker addressing large crowds at the Usher Hall often accompanied by Helen Hughes, who would speak last and give a clairvoyant demonstation to the audience. Upon the death of Arthur Conan Doyle, Swaffer was made an Honorary President of the SNU.

Maurice Barbanell (1902-1981) and Hannen were friends and for many years Swaffer's home circle was the venue for regular sittings with Maurice Barbanell. This circle is well known as the circle through which the famous Spiritual guide "Silver Birch" spoke. The medium was of course Maurice Barbanell.

'Barbie' as he was affectionately known, is the third person most closely linked with the Edinburgh College. Barbanell was a businessman turned journalist, a talented author, writing eight books on Spiritualism and through his trance mediumship a further nine books of spiritual discourses were produced. He was a frequent visitor to the Edinburgh College and a good friend of Catherine Allan. He chaired and spoke at many meetings both at the college and in the large public halls of the city. At the college he lectured and attended séances. As we have already said, Barbanell, together with Jack Rubens, Swaffer's accountant, founded Psychic News in 1932 and, with the financial backing of Arthur Findlay, became its first editor. The newspaper would often cover the activities of the Edinburgh College. Maurice Barbanell's association with the Edinburgh College lasted nearly fifty years and the service, help and advice that he freely gave the College was of huge help in

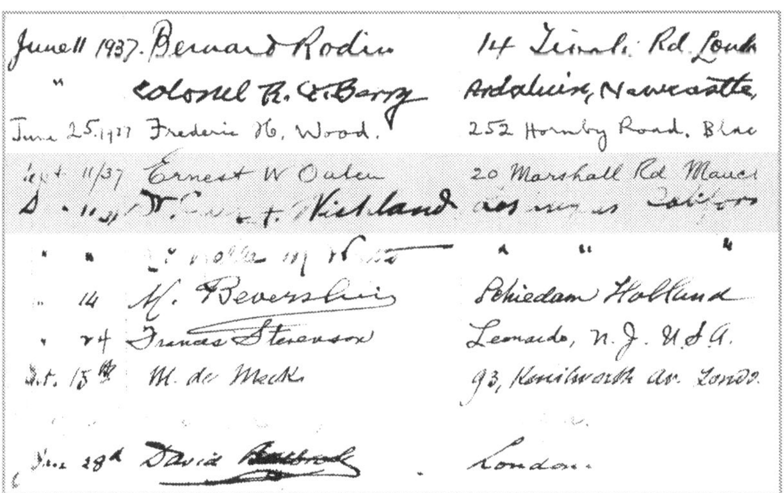
June 11 1937. Bernard Rodin — 14 [illegible] Rd. Lond.
" Colonel R. E. Barry — Andalusia, Newcastle
June 25, 1937 Frederic H. Wood. — 252 Hornby Road, Blac
Sept 11/37 Ernest W Oaten — 20 Marshall Rd Manc
[illegible] Dr. Carl A. Wickland — Los Angeles California
" " [illegible]
" 14 M. Beversluis — Schiedam Holland
" 24 Frances Stevenson — Leonardo, N. J. U.S.A.
Oct. 15th M. de Meck — 93, Kenilworth Av. London
June 28th David [illegible] — London.

Visitors' Book for 1937 -38. Amongst the visitors that year were Carl Wickland and Ernest Oaten again.

getting the new institute known and keeping the College going. He was an able publicist for the College and a good friend to its many officers.

A picture emerges of the literary connections that the new College possessed. We have already noted Swaffer, Findlay, Herries, Geraldine Cummins and Vale Owen and yet to be mentioned are several others who were writers. Rev. C. Drayton Thomas(1), Dr Nandor Fodor (researcher), James Leigh(2), Estelle Stead(3); also Richard Boddington, Dr Carl Wickland(4), Simone St.Clair, G.W. Tyrrell, another journalist and the well-known trance medium Estelle Roberts.

Of the many figures that graced the Heriot Row College it is also worth noting more occasional visitors. As well as being on the College Council and also a trustee J. B. McIndoe, was President of the SNU for 1930-38. Another frequent visitor as seen from the Visitors' Book was notable Socialist and Spiritualist SNU Past-President Ernest Oaten.

Another visiting SNU President was W. L.Haig, who addressed an AGM of the SNU in Edinburgh in July 1949 at the Music Hall, by saying that "We have been accused of trying to found a new religious sect but Spiritualism does not seek to do that, it seeks only

SNU President (1915-20, '22-23)
Ernest W. Oaten

SNU President (1948-50)
W. L. Haig

to widen knowledge of the great realm of nature." Membership of the Union, in 1949, was quoted to be 17,188 individuals with some 500 churches in affiliation.

Mme Simone St.Clair

In July of 1949 the College was to play host to the glamorous Madame Simone St.Clair. Mme. St.Clair was a war heroine and .holder of France's highest civil honour, the Legion de Honneur, and military honour the Croix de Guerre. Her visit was the cause of considerable excitement and the New Cavendish Ballroom at Toll-cross was hired for the event. An unusual feature of the visit was the use of a choir and the resident orchestra accompanied the special service. This is one of the few occasions when a divine service may have been held in connection with the College.

As were so many, Madame St.Clair was an able writer and this woman's writing still fills the shelves of many psychic libraries. Her forte was as a novelist, though frequently with a Spiritual side to the plots. It is quoted that she was also a medium. Simone St. Clair spoke of her experiences during the German occupation; of her many losses in the recent war, including that of her son. She moved the audience with the stories of the hardship of the occupation and of how this had led her into active resistance against the Nazis which led eventually to incarceration in the Ravensbruck concentration camp for women, where she had nearly died.

She was regarded as being one of France's great heroines and it was at her liberation that she had come across Spiritualist writings for the first time. She was France's representative to the International Spiritualist Federation and at the close of Madame St. Clair's speech the ever-reliable Helen Hughes gave a "clairaudient" demonstration in which many French names were quoted.

Another heroine, though this time of the Spiritualists, was Estelle Roberts. Most speakers would have been hosted at the College itself in Heriot Row but like her French colleague so great was the excitement at her visit in March 1949, that the College booked the Edinburgh Music Hall to accommodate the expected crowds eager to see the famous trance medium and to hear her guide "Red Cloud" speak. And, presumably there would have been a steady demand for private sittings in addition to the weekly demonstration.

Estelle Roberts

We know of the many famous people who visited the college from the Visitors' Book, which is still kept at the College. Of course the book gives little insight as to the purpose of their visits. Some

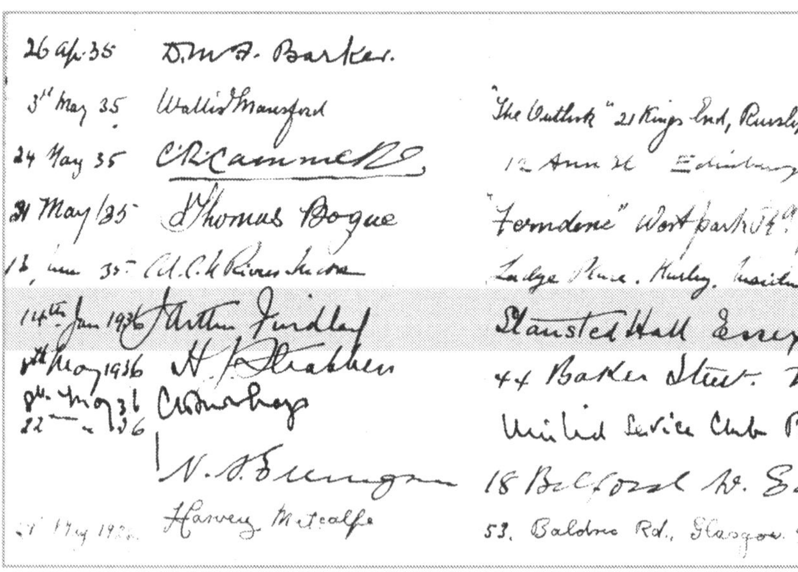

26 Apr 35 D.M.A. Barker.
3rd May 35 Wallis Mansford "The Outlook" 21 Kings End, Ruislip
24 May 35 C.R. Cammell 12 Ann St Edinburgh
31 May/35 Thomas Bogue "Ferndene" West park Rd
14th Jan 1936 Arthur Findlay Stansted Hall Essex
44 Baker Street
United Service Club
18 Belford Rd. E.
Harvey Metcalfe 53 Baldovan Rd., Glasgow

Visitors' Book for 1935, showing that Arthur Findlay visited that year but we know he was also the Speaker at a Gayfield Sq. meeting with Helen Hughes on Nov 11th 1938. (L. C-S)

we know were speaking or demonstrating on that particular date and were probably given accommodation within the College. We know the building was "roomy" and some houses in Heriot Row today are used as hotels.

Finally, in this chapter we look at the contribution made to the life of the College by those whose names go unrecorded or are hardly mentioned. These are the unsung heroes of this story. People such as the College secretary in the1950's, Mrs Simpson; Mrs Lyon, a healer from the wartime whom Mrs Allan commended in her annual speech. Other healers mentioned were Mrs Cairnduff and Mr Baker. There was a Mrs Gilhespie, briefly an Honorary Principal in 1960. Mr H. Scott Harrison, a pioneering newspaper photographer, College trustee and Council member who died in 1952. In addition there were many librarians and hall attendants who voluntarily gave of their time to ensure that a stranger would have a welcome at the door. There were many others who selflessly served to keep the College clean and made sure that a welcome cup of tea was ready after the meetings or sittings. It is these people, unknown people, who above all, deserve to be remembered for it was their service that kept the College open and its services available to the enquirer.

The other nameless supporters without whom the Psychic College and Library could not have flourished were the members. They have formed the core of support that has backed the College's activities for 75 years. Numbers have fluctuated and the actual figures are patchy, however, they do tell a story of steady support.

In 1937, 240 members are recorded. In 1938, 230 are mentioned, by the first Christmas of the War in 1939 there were 223 and in the summer of 1941, that saw Germany's invasion of Russia, it dropped to 220. The following year the figure was back up to 240. After Mrs Honywill's financial statement in 1944, the total is given as 366 members and Mrs Allan noted that this was an increase of 71 members over the previous year. Catherine Allan mentioned in an article of the mid-1950s that the college was especially busy during the war but figures for after the war are sporadic, although there may be further records in College's chaotic archives.

These archives do however give us an insight as to the finances of the college. In 1938, Mrs Miller paid a rent to live at the College of £2 per week and £2 more for a nurse to attend her. In addition the benefactor donated annually the sum of £300. Salaries in July of 1937 were found for key workers with the Secretary receiving £144, the hostess, £60 and maid and caretaker being in receipt of £48 apiece. The total being the sum of money donated by Mrs Miller i.e. Mrs Miller was paying the salaries. In addition it was noted that Miss Livingstone, the Librarian, be paid £5 per month with a further 12/6 deferred in respect of her lodgings at Heriot Row.

Mrs Miller's "generosity " was annually noted and only during the war was the sum donated by Mrs Miller reduced. Occasional sums were forthcoming, as required, and the lady gave unstintingly to her College. For example, from records in August 1940, "Mrs Miller donated extra £50", two months later, "Mrs Miller forth £114" and the list goes on from 1932 till the end of Mrs Miller's earthly days. Money was also a consideration in the College deciding to take out "Kindred Body" status with the Spiritualist National Union. The fee was small, only £4 per annum. On 17th November 1944, the Council noted that the extra protection of Union in defending, in court, their mediums might prove to be invaluable in the event of the College being sued or having to defend one of its workers. In April of 1944, at the Old Bailey in London, Victoria Helen Duncan had been found guilty of Witchcraft. Clearly the College had its eye on self-protection. Further, it was thought that the College was "dependent to a great extent on the help of the Union for engagement of visiting mediums". You will recall that Miss Mowat had said in 1960, that she would "rather see the College fold, than see it become an SNU Church". This response came about in respect of a motion at a Council meeting. The actual motion is not recorded but was probably a motion to affiliate fully to the Union. In effect become a church. A Mrs Gilhespie, the Honorary Principal may have been the instigator of the motion and resigned in the same year.

It is recorded that the Harry Edwards Healing demonstration, though this time of 1957 at the Usher Hall, generated a profit of

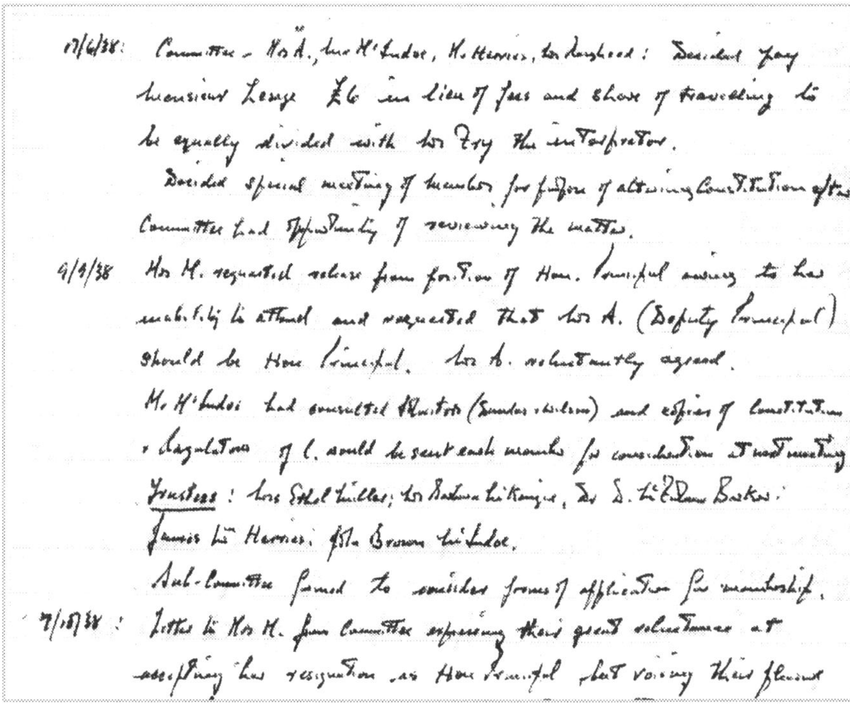

17/6/38: Committee – Mrs A., Mr McIndoe, Mr Harries, Mr [illegible]: Decided pay Monsieur Lange £6 in lieu of fees and share of travelling to be equally divided with Mr [illegible] the interpreter.
Decided special meeting of members for purpose of altering Constitution after Committee had opportunity of reviewing the matter.
9/9/38 Mrs H. requested release from position of Hon. Principal owing to her inability to attend and requested that Mr A. (Deputy Principal) should be Hon Principal. Mr A. reluctantly agreed.
Mr McIndoe had consulted [illegible] ([illegible]) and copies of Constitution & Regulations of C. would be sent each member for consideration at next meeting.
Trustees: Mrs Ethel Miller; Mr Andrew McKenzie, Dr S. McEwan Barker; James McHarries; John Brown McIndoe.
Sub-Committee formed to consider forms of application for membership.
7/10/38: Letter to Mrs H. from Committee expressing their great reluctance at accepting her resignation as Hon Principal but voicing their pleasure

Part of the first page of the handwritten notes, presumably copied, on to the foolscap sheets, from the minutes of Council meetings, these notes have beeen used for this book.

£313.7s 5d. with a donation going to the Healing Sanctuary of £75. What fee, if any, Harry Edwards took is not mentioned and it may be assumed that such would have been mentioned had one been taken. Another "Propaganda meeting" this time with Air Marshall, Lord Dowding and Sydney Peters M.P. in April of 1944 produced a profit of £266. This was underlined, so it must have been a "nice little earner". The public was charged 5/- per ticket. These large meetings did not always produce a profit and the fees paid to the speakers are quite revealing.

If a skilled working man in the 1950s was earning between £5 and £7 per week it gives us a basis for comparison, a meeting such as that given at the New Cavendish Rooms in May 1956, produced the following balance sheet. Hall rent and expenses £37, Maurice Barbanell £10/10/- with Helen Hughes receiving £ 5/5/-. The resulting profit to the College being only £13. The Teasurer was not impressed. A colleague at the Gayfield Square Spiritualist

Association suggested that they hire the Odd Fellows Hall, which would be cheaper than the New Cavendish Rooms.

Legacies were also quite common and increasingly so as the years rolled on. "Legacy £200; legacy of £100 in 1960 from J.W. Herries estate. In January 1958, there was a legacy from Mrs Alexander of 14 Belgrave Crescent of £200. (Helen Duncan gave sittings at this address which Laura Culme-Seymour attended). But it should not be thought that all was salaries and honey. Deficits were nearly as common as balances in the black. Much of Mrs Miller's generosity was needed to keep the College afloat. The war saw the College flourish but the AGM for 1940 gives a £110 deficit. Mrs M. made up the difference. After Mrs Miller's death the College kept the books balanced though seldom in a healthy profit. The notes that our scribe left behind are full of expenses. The following indicates that the Treasurer kept his eye on the purse strings. 23rd of May 1958 " Coal, gas and electricity, 1952 -£140, 1956 -£147, 1957/58 - £167. With heating for the months of Sept. to May 1958 at £120. One can almost hear the calculations going on in the man's head. With the accustomed temerity of caretakers, the resident asked for and the Council gave permission on 10th December 1958 for a T.V. aerial! The Treasurer, evidently took a dim view of the caretakers request for the aerial and used the exclamation mark in his original notes.

A motion of 28th August 1945 that did not lead to any further action was the proposed purchase of 29 Heriot Row at £3,000. The building was in need of a total refurbishment at an estimated cost of £3,000. The idea was considered, as there was a need "for a larger premises". However, it may be assumed that the extra finance was beyond the realms of possibility and the Treasurer noted nothing further. Prestige property all over the country could be had for lower than pre-war prices. The sums asked for the property are by today's prices comparatively low. However, the British economy after WWII was close to bankruptcy having mortgaged its assets to the US. to pay for WWII. Prior to the Marshall Plan, from the USA money was tight. Interestingly enough in 1972, 30 Heriot Row itself sold for only £27,000.

It is worth noting that the College and its purposes were by no

Twenty-first Anniversary Celebrations, Sept 1953

In connection with the twenty-first anniversary celebrations of the Edinburgh Psychic College a social was held in the College at 30 Heriot Row. The group includes the Council of the College:-

Mr J.W. Herries, Rev G. Morgan, Mr J..B. McIndoe

Mrs Simpson, College Sec., Helen Hughes, Mrs C. Allan, Hon.Principal, Mrs Hankey, Mrs J. Wilson, Mrs D. Wilson

Newspaper Report of the 21st Anniversary Celebrations

Growth Of Edin. Psychic College

Well-known mediums, as well as other notable figures in the psychic movement, were present at a luncheon given by the Edinburgh Psychic College on Saturday to celebrate its 21st anniversary.

Proposing the toast of the College, Mr J. W. Herries, chairman, said that the 21 years had been marked by a growing influence of the movement, and the College, from its fortuitous beginnings, had grown and firmly established itself as an institution in Edinburgh. It was one of the important organs in the advancing of psychic science throughout the country.

The essential and fundamental function of the College, h esaid, was not to spread any kind of dogma or theory, but simply to provide opportunities for people who wished to get some light on the age-long problem of whether, after a man dies, he shall live again. Conviction did not come readily by reading books although one of the other purposes of the College was to provide authoritative literature on the subject. At the College premises, at 30 Heriot Row, there existed one of the finest and most impressive collections of books on the subject to be found in this country.

SCIENTIFIC INTEREST

Although the work had been carried on for 21 years, no one, said Mr Herries, but the wildest optimist would suggest that it was completed, or even on the way to completion. The work was yet in means un-opposed. The reports have come to light that indicate a quite vociferous, if un-orchestrated, steady stream of letters of objection in the popular press to Spiritualism in general and the College in particular.

And over all this teaming activity, there presided the calm and astute Honorary Principal Mrs Catherine Allan. In 1960, Mrs Allan would have concurred with Miss Mowat, who was recorded as saying that she "would rather see the College fail, than have it turned into a Spiritualist Church". Clearly the retiring Principal felt that the proposed change would be a betrayal of Mrs Miller's vision of a non-denominational, non-religious centre that would be open to all enquirers.

In 1953, the year that Catherine celebrated 15 years as Principal, it was said of her, that she ruled with a wise supervision. That supervision had sustained the vision of Mrs Miller and taken the College through wartime and seen an extraordinary growth in the new establishment's influence and activities. Heriot Row was named in memory of a jeweller, Heriot who had worked for his patron, King James VI. In Catherine Allan, Mrs Miller had placed at the head of the College a true jewel of rare ability.

3 'Ye'll tak' the high road.....'

"O, ye'll tak' the high road and I'll tak' the low road
and I'll be in Soctland afore ye"
Anon

Many well-known people, speakers, writers, physical mediums, lecturers and prominent leaders of the Spiritualist movement made the trek from all points of the compass to "Auld Reekie" to visit and serve the only Psychic College in Scotland. It would be a challenge to find a "major" name that did not visit Edinburgh's new college. Amongst the old papers of the College one name stands out as being closely associated with the new establishment. So much so that she became a close friend of Catherine Allan and Mrs Miller.

Helen Hughes at the microphone of London's Kingsbury Hall.

"A sprightly rather frail little woman steps on to the platform, among the thousands waiting to hear her there is a hushed expectancy. Smiling, serene, confident she faces her audience with an engaging air of friendliness."

This is the opening passage of the biography of Helen Hughes who became the medium most associated with the Edinburgh Psychic College and Library but Helen was not a Scot.(1)

The medium was born on April 11th 1893 at Seaham Harbour, County Durham. Her father worked in the traditional glass making industry of Sunderland as a bottle-finisher. Her grandmother was said to be mediumistic and Helen recalls that her father's mother possessed the gifts of clairvoyance and clairaudience. Helen was predominately clairaudient. The family was Methodist and knew nothing of Spiritualism. From a child Helen saw and played with spirit children who naturally were invisible to all but her. Helen's mother told her off for telling lies "But the lovely sights of the other world were always there." Even at school she was punished for "seeing things." On one occasion twelve other children also saw the spirit of a child but the teacher punished poor little Helen as "the ring leader" of a childish practical joke.

Helen grew and married Thomas Hughes a miner of Dawdon Colliery, Co Durham, whom she had known since she was fourteen. She had three children in four years, before she was twenty-two. Before the birth of her last child she developed a severe spinal complaint and became an invalid without hope of recovery. She nearly died but wrote afterwards "for it happened when I was near the portals of death, and my friends sat around me waiting for the passing, I found myself walking in a garden of dazzling beauty when I met an elderly lady whom I knew to be long since dead." Helen was told by this deceased lady, "Not yet, you have work to do".

One day shortly afterwards, as the invalid was again getting around her small home on crutches, a road mender knocked at the door, asking to heat his tea; hesitatingly, Helen told him that she was to move as the house was haunted by an old woman. He replied in the local dialect, "Why hinney," he exclaimed, "ye're the richest woman in Dawdon! She has come to do you good, and to help you, and you are going to be a great woman".

Helen Hughes went on to address capacity audiences at the Royal Albert Hall in London and several times, at the behest of the College, filled the Usher Hall in Edinburgh with 3000 people. In 1944, at the Usher Hall, with a packed house, and some 300 turned away, the Moderator of the Church of Scotland the Rev. Maclean chaired while Maurice Barbanell gave a spirited defence of

Spiritualism and Helen Hughes, delivered the messages of survival from members of the armed forces who had passed on into the Spirit World. She went on to be one of the most engaged of all speakers of the Edinburgh College.

Maurice Barbanell speaking at the microphone of the Usher Hall, Edinburgh while Helen Hughes waits to give the proof of survival. 1943

Soon after the College opened in September 1932, Helen Duncan was invited to give a series of test séances. The arrangements were that Duncan would be paid 2 guineas for the sitting, whereas, the College would gather in 10 shillings per sitter. How many of these might have received discount, or be given free places if they were College officials, is not clarified. On the face of it, Helen Duncan was not being over paid. It would appear that as a result of these sittings she insisted on being given half the door receipts and this was agreed. Folklore has it that Helen Duncan considered the College to be "Hoity-toity".

Victoria Helen Duncan's relationship had not, in the first five months of the College's existence, been easy. Money was the root of the problem but as ever a compromise was struck and the alliance with the College was resumed and continued for 18 years up to 1950, which is the last time we have a record of a Helen Duncan séance at the Heriot Row College.

The same problem of payment arose with the Spiritualist National Union, which was also, in effect, under-paying the medium and keeping anything up to 80% of the fees. After a bitter dispute the Union refused to pay more and the medium and Union parted company forever. Maurice Barbanell warned Helen that the protection of the Union was important to her and not to over tax her strength by giving too many séances. Helen's family was large; she suffered the death of several infants and her husband Henry was frequently ill. The medium needed to be working. Her daughter, Gina Brealey, in her book "The Two Worlds of Helen Duncan" comments that Helen Duncan would give services "free to churches and people in need of guidance, but too poor to pay".

On 21st of January 1938, it was decided by the Council that Helen Hughes should receive the same fee in Edinburgh as she was accustomed to getting in London, 10/-, with a College member paying 15/- and a non-member 17/6 for entrance. The discount thereby was an encouragement to the public to take up membership of the College. It was decided also that Helen Duncan would be given half of the fee paid for photographs taken at her séances, with 4 copies reserved for the College. Unfortunately none of these photos has survived in the archives.

Trumpet movement during a trance demonstration by Helen Duncan, 1949

Photographs which have survived elsewhere have freqequently given rise to questions concerning the validity of some of Helen's materialisations but Alan Crossley, who sat with her a number of times, gives this explanation in his book about her mediumship.(2)

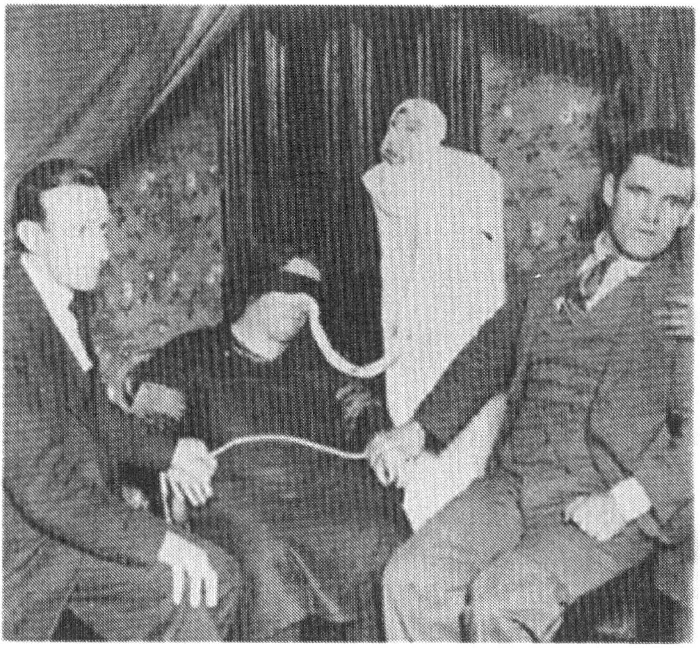

Plate 4.
A more substantial form is produced. At this stage, the purpose is to manipulate and mould the ectoplasm and perfect the process of reproducing as near a likeness of the deceased person as possible. The infusion of the animating force, the spirit, gives the form the ability to speak and hold a normal, intelligent conversation as well as appearing to resemble the person whom they claim to be.

Note the rope-like cord which links the form to the medium. With a full materialization, the medium has been known to lose a considerable amount of weight.

Explanation, by Alan Crossley (on the right of the medium) of the development of a materialised form in Helen Duncan's séances.

The College also offered a transcription service. In October 1938, in response from the public for transcripts of their sittings the Council agreed to buy a typewriter and to charge 5/- for a copy. I am pleased to say that within the archives of the College, I have found three of a set of five 78 rpm. records of a Helen Duncan séance. These may have been used to provide a transcript for the sitters.

Helen Duncan's presence at the Edinburgh College may be seen as a precedent by which physical mediumship continues to be demonstrated in the present day with physical mediums Colin Fry having held physical séances there since 2000, Stewart Alexander since 2005 and Ray Smith demonstrating trance, but more of them later.

We don't know how frequently Helen Duncan came to the Edinburgh College but we do know that she gave regular séances at the College for eight years from 1932 until 1940 and that she was again at the College in 1950. The College records for the 1940s are incomplete and don't mention her at all. However the College's entry in 'The Manual and Who's Who of Spiritualism and Psychic Research for 1936' states that:-

"Materialisation séances,--Mrs Helen Duncan of Edinburgh will conduct group séances at the College once or twice per week at the College whenever she is available. Members, 10s 6d and non-members 12s 6d."

Whereas, the College provided a séance facility as part of its services, it nevertheless should be noted that to many Spiritualists, the purpose of the séance was not simply to see Spirit materialised it was to experience matter spiritualised. i.e. to demonstrate that the temporal was but an extension of the spiritual. There are no references to Helen nor anyone else giving physical séances to individuals. It may have been possible for a group to book a private séance though there is no evidence of that occurring within the College. Small private séances were held in peoples' homes, as we know from the records of Mrs Culme- Seymour in her book, and it was because of one of these private séances that the medium had her first brush with the law.

On 16th March 1933, at the Edinburgh Magistrate's court, Helen Duncan (1898-1956) was arraigned and ordered to appear again before the court, *sine die*, to reply to the charge of Fraud. She was to answer that charge in front of Sheriff Macdonald at the

Edinburgh Sheriff's Court on Wednesday the 3rd of May 1933.

The famous medium was charged that she had, at her Craigmillar home in the suburbs of the city and in Stafford Street, organised séances at which, it was reported, "she pretended to eight persons that she was a medium through whom the spirits of deceased persons were openly and regularly materialised in such a manner as to be visible to, to speak to, and converse with those present in the room". As the law of Scotland did not recognise that such a thing was possible, Helen Duncan must therefore be guilty. She was fined 10 shillings.

The accounts that follow are the records of sittings which Mrs Laura Culme-Seymour attended and they give us some idea of the work done at the College. Through her accounts, we have first hand testimony of one of the great physical mediums, Helen Duncan, of what that mediumship was and what it meant to be one of the sitters. In addition, Mrs Culme-Seymour has left us records of the other mediums with whom she sat, and through her records something of their work has come down to posterity. We are indebted to the lady for keeping a record of her sittings, which was used as the resource for her book, 'Marjorie' from which these details are taken; a signed copy of which is in the College Library.

Marjorie Culme-Seymour, Autumn 1933

On 21st January 1934, Marjorie, the lovely teenage daughter of Cmdr. Evelyn Culme-Seymour RN and his wife Laura, drowned while out in a canoe. The Culme-Seymours were strong Christians but in December of 1936, following a number of successful visits by Mrs Culme-Seymour to the College and privately to mediums, Marjorie's parents went to a public demonstration of clairvoyance at the College given by the ever-popular Helen Hughes. The famous speaker described the couple's daughter..." I see a beautiful girl, grey blue-eyes, very bright expression, she says it's Marjorie". (3)

There followed a series of group sittings sometimes with Helen Hughes and sometimes with Edith Potts, who also gave private trance sittings at the College. On all these occasions Laura Culme-Seymour says good evidential messages were given.

On 6th March 1937 Mrs Culme-Seymour, with a friend, attended her first materialisation séance at the college with Helen Duncan ".... and I must honestly say I was very nervous about it." She describes the pre-sitting preparation thus, "Two women who had never seen Mrs Duncan before went to see her undressed and she put on black stockings, black knickers and a black overall. These ladies vouched that Mrs Duncan had nothing white on or about her. My friend and I both examined the "cabinet" and can testify that there was nothing there but a chair. Mrs Duncan went behind the curtain and sat on the chair and then a man's voice (Albert, her control) spoke - just before he came we all said the Lord's Prayer. Albert was a tall figure in a white robe, he opened the curtain and stepped out and showed himself."

Helen Duncan's guide 'Albert' who conducted the progress of a séance.

The séance progressed, with several forms coming forward to be seen, sometimes speaking for themselves but occasionally Albert spoke for them. Sometimes Albert relayed messages from the departed

The ectoplasm starts to flow from Helen Duncan's nostril. Alan Crossley, the researcher, sits to her right.

who were not materialised in the room. The narrative picks up with the following, "Albert pointed at me and said. "There is a young lady wanting to show herself, it was a very sudden passing, she was in radiant health, she was never ill. Will the lady speak to her?" I was terribly nervous, but knew it was our beloved child and managed to control myself and said, "Is that you, my darling, do come and show yourself." The curtain then parted and Marjorie stepped out in a long white robe. A torch was then given to the materialised form who flashed it several times on her own face. Laura Culme-Seymour goes on to say, "I am sure it was her, but she could only stay a few seconds."

Mrs Culme-Seymour was to have more than 12 sittings with Helen Duncan and at one point in her book she offered this interesting portrait of the famous medium. "Mrs Duncan is a big, rather fat woman with a Scottish accent, none of the voices were in the least like hers. We were in the dark except for a red light but could make out each other's faces. It was certainly a very wonderful and unforgettable experience".

She continues, "I think the greatest miscarriage of justice of which I've ever heard, was the conviction and imprisonment of Mrs

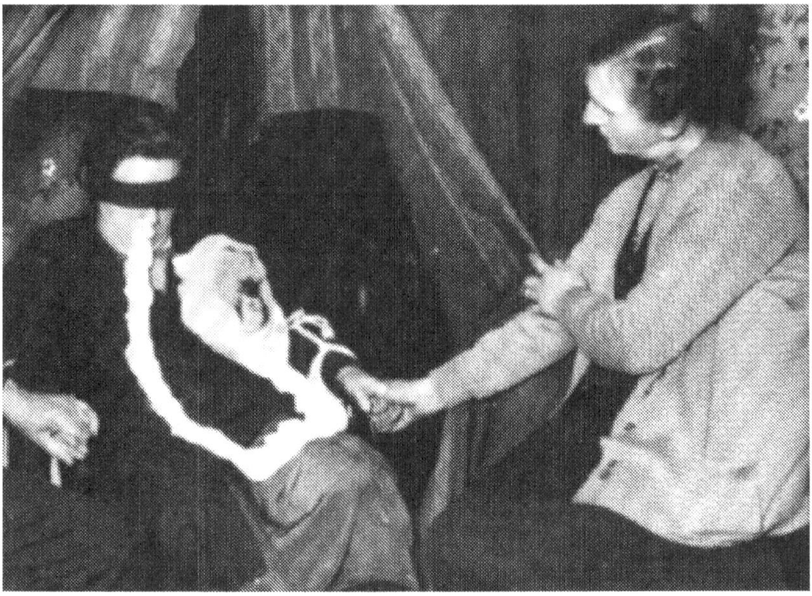

The ectoplasm is formed into a man's face against Helen Duncan's shoulder.

Duncan. She had given a sitting in Portsmouth. The accuser said she had concealed white muslin and somehow arranged it to represent figures. It was all too ridiculously impossible. At all the sittings I was at Mrs Duncan was always taken to a private room where, before two of the women of the circle, she undressed and put on black stockings, knickers and an overall. There was no possibility of her concealing anything white anywhere."

Laura was to sit at least twice in October of 1937, with Helen Duncan, one sitting taking place at the Edinburgh Psychic College and Library. On each occasion Marjorie communicated, as did other figures known to Laura Culme-Seymour. The following account during a private séance at Mrs Roughhead's is of particular interest for the details it gives us of Helen Duncan's mediumship.

"Great clouds of ectoplasm coming from Mrs Duncan still in deep trance and a large psychoplastic rod which he (Albert) asked me to stand on. It felt like rubber and quite lifted my foot. Then he dematerialised Mrs Duncan, who completely disappeared - we saw her getting smaller and smaller. A long table was lifted up...it was indeed a wonderful afternoon."

When Hannen Swaffer sat with Helen Duncan at the College he was also allowed to touch, with the permission of the spirit guides, the ectoplasm coming from the medium. On some occasions his friends on the "other side of life" were able to shake his hand and talk to the journalist. These conversations, he later stated, involved matters that could only have been known to himself. He asserted that the hands always felt real and warm.[(4)]

Laura had found in the materialisation sittings a renewed interest. The very thought of going to another sitting in November 1938 brought forth this response :-

"I was so thrilled with the materialisation sittings that I had been to, that when I heard there was to be another one at the College on the 15th I felt I must go, and was indeed rewarded. Several figures showed themselves and on this occasion Albert again called for a torch, one was produced, "Marjorie came out flashing the torch on her face and looking quite radiant. She showed herself twice and her most beautiful shining robes and said how she loved to come and was pleased that I had come. It was all so wonderful and one could hardly believe one had really been privileged to see this".

Laura Culme-Seymour did not have to be present at a Helen Duncan séance for Marjorie to make her presence known, as she records. "On 1st March I telephoned a friend and had a long talk. That evening the friend went along to a materialisation séance with Helen Duncan at the College". We are told that Marjorie again materialised and said she had been so interested in the telephone conversation that her mother had with her friend that morning.

The accounts speak of various other sittings with mediums at the College, notably Helen Hughes and Edith Potts. Further sittings at the Edinburgh College were sought and paid for with a Mrs Edith Thomson and with a Mrs Stevenson of New Jersey, USA.

Mrs Culme-Seymour sat with a Mrs Kelly who gave a trance sitting at the College in which her daughter spoke through the medium and in September 1938 she sat with Kathleen Barkel who gave her excellent personal evidence, while in trance, and allowed

Kathleen Barkel

Marjorie to speak through her and Marjorie gave her mother advance news of the birth of a baby girl to her sister, Rosie.

Kathleen Barkel worked as a medium at the Marylebone Spiritual Association in London and when asked about her mediumship she said "I fell asleep in front of the fire in 1922 and I've been going off to sleep ever since". (*report in 'The Daily Mail', Nov.14th 1938*).

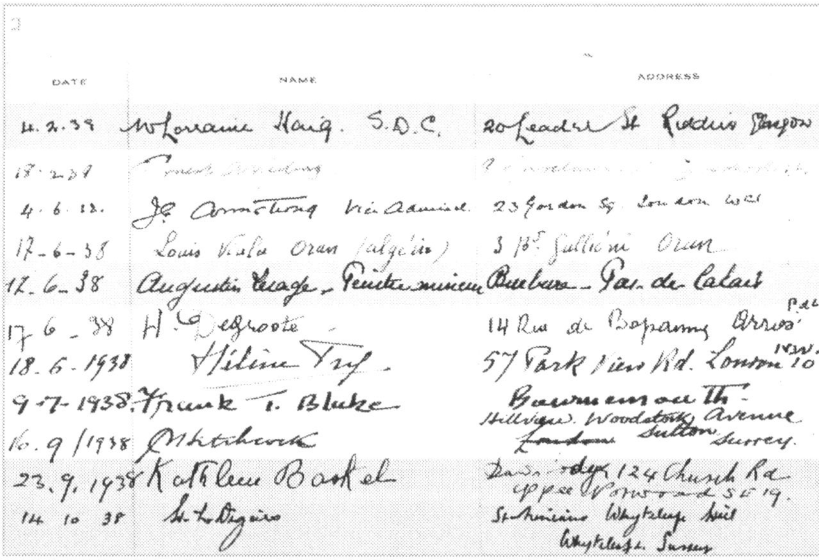

DATE	NAME	ADDRESS
4.2.38	W Lorraine Haig. S.D.C.	20 Leader St Riddrie Glasgow
18·2·38	[illegible]	[illegible]
4·6·38.	J G Armstrong Vice Admiral.	23 Gordon Sq London WC1
17-6-38	Louis Viala Oran (algérie)	3 Bd Galliéni Oran
17-6-38	Augustin Lesage - Peintre mineur	Burbure - Pas de Calais
17 6 - 38	H Degroote	14 Rue de Bapaume Arras P.dC
18-6-1938	Hélène Tryf	57 Park View Rd. London NW.10
9-7-1938.	Frank T. Blake	Bournemouth -
16.9/1938	J Hitchcock	Hillview. Woodstock Avenue ~~London~~ Sutton Surrey.
23.9.1938	Kathleen Barkel	[illegible] 124 Church Rd Upper Norwood SE19.
14 10 38	[illegible]	[illegible] Whyteleafe Hill Whyteleafe. Surrey

Page from the Visitors' Book for 1938 showing, amongst others, the visits that year of Kathleen Barkel, Harold Vigurs, W.L.Haig and Augustine Lesage.

The following month Laura Culme-Seymour also had a private trance sitting with Lilian Bailey who, according to the Visitors' Book, was demonstrating at the College with Harold Vigurs who was an accomplished speaker from Croydon.

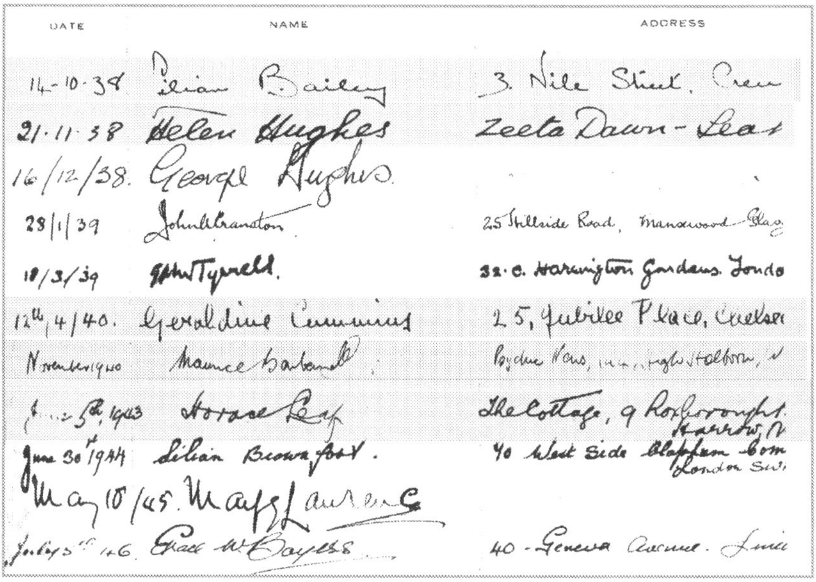

DATE	NAME	ADDRESS
14-10-38	Lilian Bailey	3. Nile Street, Crew[illegible]
21-11-38	Helen Hughes	Zeeta Dawn-Leaf
16/12/38.	George Hughes	
28/1/39	John Cranston	25 Hillside Road, [illegible] Glasg[illegible]
18/3/39	[illegible] Tyrrell.	32 c. Harrington Gardens, Londo[illegible]
12th/4/40.	Geraldine Cummins	2 5, Jubilee Place, Chelsea
November 1940	Maurice Barbanell	[illegible] High Holborn, [illegible]
June 5th 1943	Horace Leaf	The Cottage, 9 Roxborough [illegible] Harrow, [illegible]
June 30th 1944	Lilian Brownfoot.	40 West Side Clapham Com London SW[illegible]
May 10/45.	Mary Lawrence	
July 5th 46.	Grace [illegible]	40 - Geneva Avenue. [illegible]

Page from the Visitors' Book for 1938-46 showing the visits of Lilian Bailey, several of the College's famous friends, Helen Hughes, Geraldine Cummins, Maurice Barbanell and in '43 a visit from Horace Leaf.

Left:- Lilian Bailey. Awarded the OBE for service during WW1 in France. She developed her mediumship with the help of Billy Hope. A wonderful Trance and clairvoyant medium for over 40 years.(5)

Right:- Harold Vigurs. President of the SNU 1943-48, he worked hard for the repeal of the Witchcraft Act. He had a strong mystical side and was much sort after as a Speaker. (6)

Horace Leaf. A world traveller for Spiritualism, his gifts included healing, clairvoyance, trance and ,for a short time, Materialisation Phenomena. He wrote an excellent book, "What Mediumship Is" (7)

Mrs MacCallum, of Craigleith, Edinburgh was another medium with whom Laura sat a number of times, and who also gave private trance demonstrations. At one such private sitting Rudyard Kipling communicated, gave evidence of survival and conveyed his knowledge of Laura's friendship with his sister who had helped Laura Culme-Seymour understand psychic matters.

The Mrs MacCallum (of Glasgow) mentioned in chapter one, as being a physical medium attached to the College, is not the Mrs MacCallum in the previous paragraph. Mrs MacCallum of Glasgow was a Direct-Voice medium who attended the College frequently and gave direct-voice séances for some years. This medium's entry in the 'Manual and Who's Who for 1936', shows the following entry:-

"Direct-Voice séances, - It is hoped that arrangements can be made for Mrs MacCallum, of Glasgow, to attend the college once per month during this session."

The following accounts of this lady's mediumship are the only ones that have been found so far. Laura Culme-Seymour attended 5 sittings with her in two years and wrote, "In February 1937 there was to be a direct voice sitting at the College, so I decided to go. There were eleven of us including two men". A friend of MrsMacCallum, a Mrs Barr, was one of those present and her son, who had been killed in France, spoke in a very clear voice. Quite a number of characters spoke, some were taken by the recipients and some were not. However, in due course the following took place, "I heard a voice say "Amy," and I asked if it was for me and was told, "Yes, I'm Mother," and she talked a little and said, "Angus is here". I asked if she knew how he had passed over and she said "He was killed in France, I can't remember where." I cannot honestly say I would have recognised mother's voice, but I knew it was her. Quite at the end a voice said "...its Marjorie" and said something about Rosemary but I couldn't hear much". The author comments that the other sitters were given messages and that the evidence was good.

A year later Laura again attended a Direct Voice sitting with Mrs MacCallum at the College and this is her report "....the room was dark but on this occasion the medium was not in trance. After several spirits had made themselves known, a man spoke and Mrs MacCallum thought he wished to speak to me. He said his name was Angus, my brother, he rather had difficulty speaking He said, your daughter is here but I can't get her name. He then spelt out "Marjorie" and said she would speak later." The spirit gave the further proof of his identity and indicated that he knew one of the other sitters a Mr McKillop, with whom he had played the pipes...... Marjorie came later and said "Mother it's me, I'm here, Uncle Angus was speaking to you." I asked if she had seen her brother Gerald and she said "Yes in Australia, is in New Zealand now, is very happy, will be married soon." She spoke of her pearls and ring that I had on and said that I had not got her watch, she had it on when she had drowned. I asked her who had given her the watch and she spelled out Steuart, all correct. (The medium, Bertha Harris was a sitter and had seen Marjorie clairvoyantly and described her to me exactly after the sitting).

After that a Major Scott came through in his aeroplane. An amazing sound in the quiet room - he had been killed in a crash. After this Robert Louis Stevenson came and Mrs Roughhead, one of the circle, said, "You used to live near here." and he replied, "Yes at No **. (Heriot Row) and then recited "The Lamplighter". It was a wonderful sitting and I only wish some of my sceptical friends could have been there.

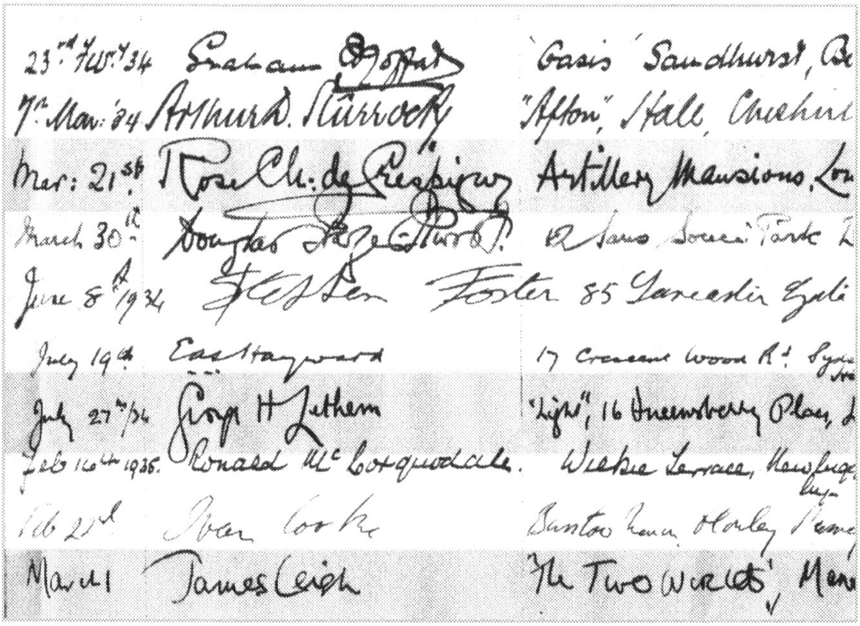

23rd Feb. '34 Graham Moffat 'Oasis' Sandhurst, ...
7th Mar: '34 Arthur D. Sturrock "Afton" Hale, Cheshire
Mar: 21st Rose Ch. de Crespigny Artillery Mansions, Lon...
March 30th Douglas ... 12 Sans Souci Park ...
June 8th 1934 ... Foster 85 Lancaster ...
July 19th ... Hayward 17 ... Wood Rd ...
July 27/34 George H Lethem "Light", 16 Queensberry Place, ...
Feb 16th 1935 Ronald Mc Corquodale. ... Terrace, ...
Feb 21st Ivan Cooke ... Horley ...
March 1 James Leigh "The Two Worlds", Man...

Page of the Visitors' Book for 1934-35 showing the visits of Rose Ch. de Crespigny, Barbara McKenzie's colleague at the British Psychic College in London, George Lethem of the publication 'Light' and in March '35 James Leigh, the Editor of 'Two Worlds'

The last sitting that Laura Culme-Seymour had notes about was one at the College on the 18th of November 1950 when she again sat with Helen Duncan. "There were ten sitters. She went in to a deep trance and we sang 'The Lord is my Shepherd' and then Albert's voice was heard greeting us all. Several people materialised and were recognised and then Albert said I would like the lady near the cabinet (which was me) to speak to someone. I said "Is it Marjorie?" She came out and showing me to the others said. "This is my mother…It's lovely to have seen you, you haven't been lately."

When writing her book in 1957 Laura concluded "It is very difficult to give an idea of what these sittings are like, but indeed it is a never to be forgotten experience and my heart is full of gratitude to the almighty God for all that I have been allowed to see and hear".

In addition to the above mediums, it was noted in an 'aside' in the 'minutes' of 12th January 1945, that a Mrs S. Leigh, a Direct

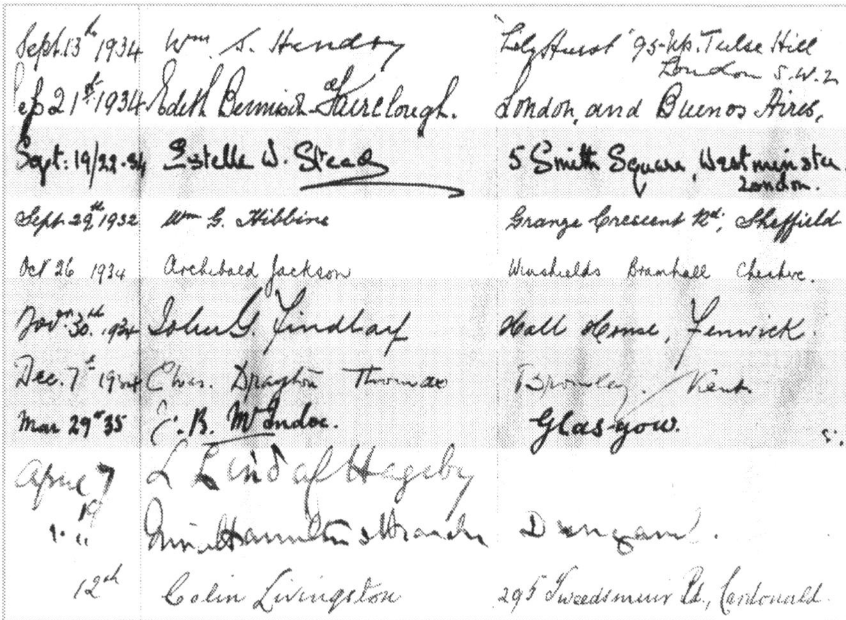

Sept 13th 1934	Wm S. Hendry	Lilyhurst 95 Up. Tulse Hill London S.W.2
Sep 21st 1934	Edith Bernice Fairclough.	London, and Buenos Aires.
Sept: 19/22.34	Estelle W. Stead	5 Smith Square, Westminster. London.
Sept 29th 1932	Wm G. Hibbins	Grange Crescent Rd; Sheffield
Oct 26 1934	Archibald Jackson	[illegible] Bramhall Cheshire.
Nov 30th 1934	John G. Findlay	[illegible], Fenwick.
Dec. 7th 1934	Chas. Drayton Thomas	Bromley, Kent
Mar 29th 35	J.B. McIndoe.	Glasgow.
April 7	L. Lind af Hageby	
10 "	[illegible]	[illegible]
12th	Colin Livingston	295 Tweedsmuir Rd., Cardonald.

This and the page opposite are dated for the same period so the visitors must have written straight across the book. This page shows the visits of Estelle Stead, John Findlay (Arthur Findlay's brother), Rev Charles Drayton Thomas and J.B. McIndoe who was a trustee of the College - all well-known speakers.

Voice medium was to give sittings fortnightly at the College to members. On the 12th of December 1956, Ivy Northage was engaged to demonstrate Transfiguration.

Some charges for sittings were listed on 16th of February 1959. I have added the prices for 1938 in brackets after them for comparison. Private sittings for clairvoyance, 15/- (15/-) and £1/1/- (17/-) to non-members, with groups costing 3/6d and 5/- per person respectively, no group-sitting price was quoted for 1938. As the figure shows no change in respect of the member's fee to be paid and only 3/6d increase for non-members, it's a fair assumption that the fee paid to the medium showed little or no increase either. What percentage was paid to the medium is not stated but one example was given in the 1930s of 10/- or two thirds of the overall fee charged. With the exigencies of the war pressing upon the population the College decided it would give 'the needy' free private sittings.

Rev Maurice Elliot. A moving force in persuading the Church of England to look into Spiritualism. He was Secretary to the Churches' Fellowship. For 53 years he used his pen and voice to broadcast the truth of proved survival and he communicated after death through the medium Ena Twigg to his friend Col. Lester.(8)

Estelle Stead with a 'spirit extra' image of her father, the journalist, who was lost with the Titanic, (Photo by Billy Hope.) She was an excellent Speaker and carried on the work of running the W.T.Stead Memorial Library and Bureau in London for 22 years. This 'Membership' Library contained books on spiritualism and kindred subjects.(9)

However, the "names" within the movement could name their own fee and in 1938 Helen Hughes was paid 15/- per private sitting, as was Ena Twigg. Edith Potts and Mrs Thomson received 12/6 each. We assume that the proportion paid to the medium remained at two thirds with one third going to the College. We don't know, nor is it mentioned whether the medium was paid travelling expenses on top of their fee, though it seems likely that they would have received out of pocket expenses. Finally, on 24th of November 1963, with the Beatles hitting the charts for the first time, the fee to sit with Helen Hughes was raised to £2/2/-. with fees for Ena Twigg and Mrs Thomson being pegged at 15/-. We know that Helen Hughes served the College for over 30 years coming to Edinburgh in 1964, missing 1965 and made her final visit in 1966, being 'promoted to the Higher Side of Life' in 1967 at the age of 74.

Also recorded in the hand-written pages our scribe outlines an area of investigation that has more to do with what is nowadays regarded as the paranormal. In the summer of 1940 as the Germans marched into France, at the Edinburgh College the Council decided upon a "Special Council for the Investigation of Abnormal Happenings". This Council, pithily, if less sympathetically known today as "Ghost Busters" was created and "appointed" by the College "to record events considered to be abnormal or unusual, without embellishment." J.W. Herries, the eminent journalist and College Council member was appointed chairman. In short, teams from the College would go out and watch and record what they found in the places they were asked to investigate. In addition, this sub-Council would give talks on subjects such as Poltergeist, ghostly appearances, sensory perceptions, etc. The object of this clumsily entitled sub-Council was "The collection and investigation of Psychic Phenomena". It was in part an attempt to return to Hewat Mackenzie's original concept of a College that would investigate all phenomena and embrace the Psychic Research aspect of Spiritualism that had become over looked in the success of the College's early years.

Of course, as ever, the College's close friend, Helen Hughes was

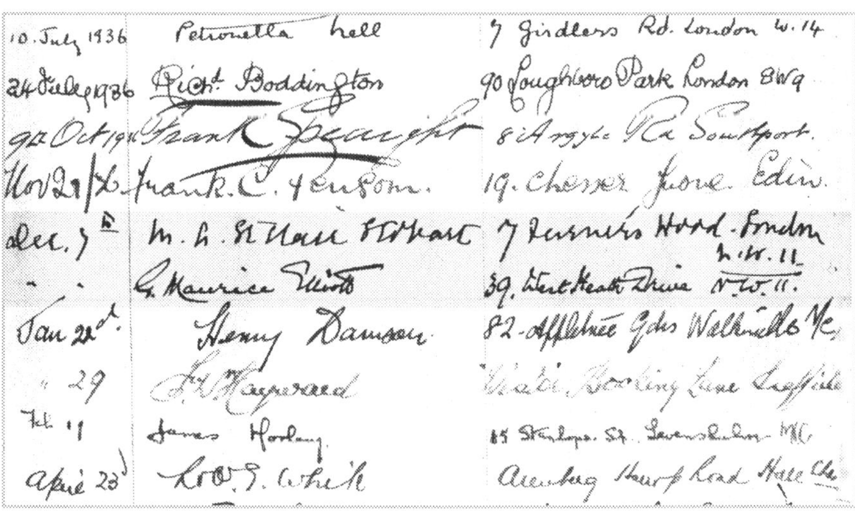

10. July 1936	Petronella [illegible]	7 Girdlers Rd. London W.14
24 July 1936	Richd Boddington	90 Loughboro Park London SW9
9th Oct 1936	Frank Speaight	8 Argyle Rd Southport.
Nov 21/36	Frank C. [illegible]	19. Chester Grove Edin.
Dec. 7th	M. A. St Clair Stobart	7 Turner's Wood. London N.W.11
"	G. Maurice Elliott	39. West Heath Drive N.W.11.
Jan 22nd	Henry Dawson	82 Appletree Gdns [illegible]
" 29	[illegible]	[illegible]
Feb 11	James [illegible]	85 Stanhope St. [illegible]
April 23	[illegible]	[illegible]

Page of the Visitors' Book for 1936-37. Rev Maurice Elliot, Marie St Clair Stobart, the author of the Healing Hymn 'Loving Father, Hear us' and Richard Boddington were among the visiting Speakers in that period.

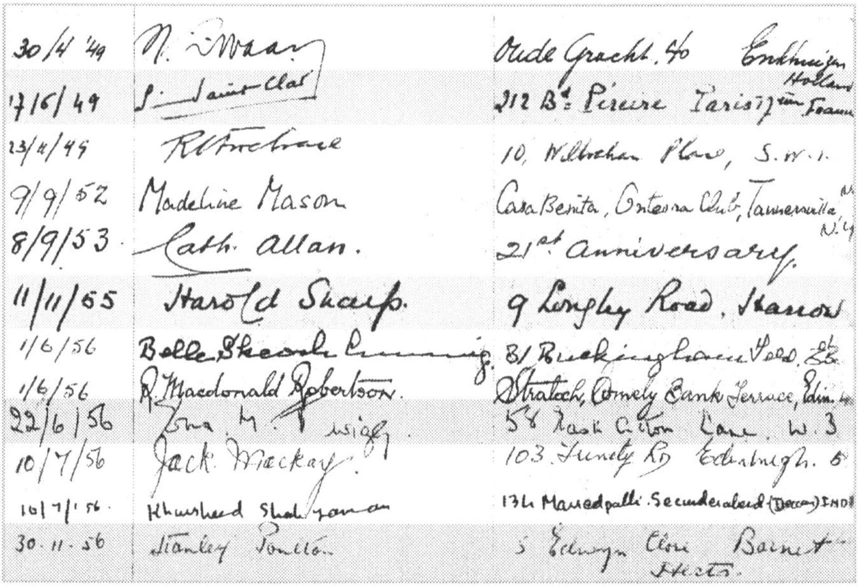

30/4 '49	N. [illegible]	Oude Gracht. 40 Enkhuizen Holland
17/6/49	S. Saint Clair	212 Bd Pereire Paris 17 France
23/4/49	[illegible]	10, Wilbraham Place, S.W.1
9/9/52	Madeline Mason	Casa Benita, Onteora Club, Tannersville N.Y.
8/9/53	Cath. Allan.	21st anniversary.
11/11/55	Harold Sharp.	9 Langley Road, Stanmore
1/6/56	Belle Skeoch Cumming	81 Buckingham Terr. Edin
1/6/56	R. Macdonald Robertson	Stratoch, Comely Bank Terrace, Edin. 4
22/6/56	Ena M. Twigg	58 [illegible] Acton Lane. W.3
10/7/56	Jack Mackay	103 Trinity Rd Edinburgh. 6
10/7/56	Khursheed [illegible]	136 [illegible] Secunderabad (Deccan) INDIA
30.11.56	Stanley Poulton	5 Edwyn Close Barnet Herts.

The page of the Visitors' Book for 1949-56 shows the signatures of Simone St Clair, the French Resistance heroine, who visited in 1949; Harold Sharp who came to the College in 1955 and mediums Ena Twigg and Stanley Poulton who gave their services there in 1956.

Ena Twigg, world reknowned Trance and mental medium who worked for many years at the London College of Psychic Studies and in the USA.(11)

Stanley Poulton, an accomplished Trance speaker and clairvoyant medium on both sides of the atlantic, through whom 'Chang' his Chinese guide communicated.(10)

on hand to lead the ghost busters boldly into new realms. In January 1942 'Two Worlds' published a pamphlet. In one case, which was investigated, the ghost of a gray lady repeatedly appeared at a house recently occupied by a well-known Scottish clergyman. The occupants had seen the figure on various occasions. Helen Hughes was taken along to the premises as medium and was able to contact the gray lady whose identity she revealed. It was found that the gray lady was an old nurse who had attended the family. Spiritualists would regard the work of this Council as "rescue work" intervening to free the souls who are "stuck" in certain temporal situations. This is regarded by Spiritualists as the other world origin of much poltergeist phenomena that was little understood by the outside world.

William Redmond :- visited Edinburgh a number of times in 1950s but eventually the Council decided his fees were too high. He developed as a medium in his late teens after investigating it following his father's death. (12) *He was particularly good at psychometry and devoted his life to propagating the philosophy and teachings of Spiritualism*(13)

Throughout this chapter the wealth of talent by the way of Speakers or Demonstrators which was made available for those searchers in need of comfort or understanding during the first 25 years of the College would take some matching in the next 50 years. We know that many of the well-known names would have continued to come to the College and others would have joined their ranks but unfortunately we haven't the records to be able continue with our parade of visitors so we must draw this section to a close.

Harold Sharp visited Edinburgh on Nov 11th 1955, presumably for the Remembrance Meeting.
Once a Roman Catholic he only looked into Evidence of Survival on behalf of a distraught friend.. (14)
As well as being a good medium for over 50 years his particular forte was in channelling delicately coloured aura-graphs from an artist named Chan Shih.

Right:-An auragraph done by Chan Shih, using Harold Sharp, in 1953 for Tom Harrison. A written interpretation was also given to the recipient. Unfortunately we are unable to show the delicate colours.

It is only appropriate that Mrs Laura Culme-Seymour who has, through her writing, given so much to this chapter should conclude it with her reason for writing the book about her daughter's 'return'.

"My only wish is to help someone suffering from an overwhelming loss such as ours, and if I can bring comfort to anyone, my labour will not have been in vain. I thank God for His goodness in leading me to so many wonderful mediums, and for the inspiration I have received"

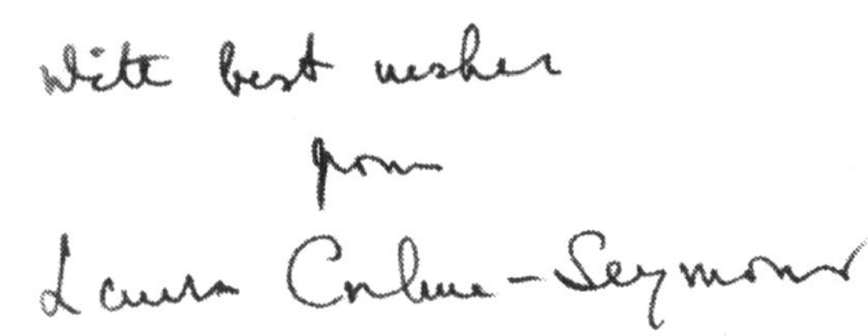

Inscription from the fly-leaf of Laura's book 'Marjorie', which is in the College library.

4 *'My old man said follow the van . . . .'*

"We packed all that could be packed in the van and that's a fact;
And we got inside all we could get inside;"
Charles Collins and Fred Leigh

Transitions and difficulties surmounted often have the net effect of giving a venture new life and revitalising tired spirits. Following the death of Mrs Miller no patron had stepped forward to help bank-roll the College. The period of 1946 to 1972 had seen the College flourish and then decline. The 1960s in particular saw many of the well known names closely associated with the College pass "to the higher side of life". Perhaps the psychic quest had ceased to enthral the public as once it had done. The very idea of a psychic college came to appear old fashioned.

Yet the 1960s had seen the College continue to provide its services to the public. And quite a cast of mediums filled its platform. Throughout the decade certain names crop up frequently and other names disappear. The names of those who passed on in the 1960s would be a long one and there is no need to dwell on this theme, except to note that Catherine Allan and Edith Potts as well as others already mentioned, all left the scene to a younger generation. Lists of serving mediums and speakers are given in the Appendices. Among the stalwarts who are fondly remembered were Mrs Jean Thompson, Ivy Gilhespie, Mrs Lexie Finlater, Agnes Porter, Cecily Moore and Nan Livingstone. It is recorded that Mrs Gilhespie of Glasgow was clairaudient and gave talks on different topics before her demonstration whereas, Mrs Findlater, who lived down at Grangemouth, was clairvoyant. In later years, also warmly remembered is Minister Mary Duffy, an Edinburgh resident, who served the College through three decades. Mary died in 2005, still travelling and working. Another who served the College for many years and fondly remembered is Clem' Harvey, who died in 2004.

The College continued to provide other services. It was customary for the College to present a talk prior to the mediumistic demonstration and it is still the practice to have such a talk before each meeting. In the 1960s talks were given on many subjects; 8th February 1962, Mrs Ruth Brasted spoke on the "Aquarian Foundations of the Living God". On the 19th September 1969, Rev. Donald MacKay, addressed the topic of "The Practical Value of Other Worldliness".

In keeping with the College's ethos, two weeks later, on 3rd October, Mr E. Symonds gave a talk on "Man Know Thyself", which of course the Greek philosopher Plato, had inscribed above the entry to his school of philosophy. This most apt of instruction was part and parcel of Spiritualist practice; the study of which had brought the College into being. For without the going within, there could be no knowledge and such knowledge was thought to come upon the medium in the manner of a leading out of that which is within. As quoted in 'The Prime of Miss Jean Brodie', "Education is a leading out, from e, out and duco, I lead."

Later that month a Mr F.W. Hay gave the qualifications after his name as MSIPME what this impressive string of letters represented sadly we have not been able to establish but no doubt his talk and subsequent discussion on "Mind and Body" was well received as the gentleman visited on further occasions. The lecture was still the order of the day and judging by their frequency and topics covered they must have been popular and well supported. They were nearly always followed by a demonstration of 'mediumship' with the clairaudient often being described in the Syllabus with a continental flourish as "clairaudiente".

One can almost hear the chink of cutlery on china at the College Coffee mornings held on Saturdays, at 10.30, with an accompanying 'Cake and Candy stall', admission was three shillings. Other activities included Wednesdays "Discussion and Research Group at 7.30p.m, Members only". The College healers were available for private treatments "by appointment". There was an open night held monthly for non-members and in the mid-sixties a Mrs Kesson ran a "Developing group" which non-members could attend. It was all beginning to sound a little tired, a little staid.

The College had survived into the age of the cultural revolutions of the 1960s. During the "Summer of Love" in 1967, Jimmy Hendrix was singing "Purple haze going round in my brain", which contrasted sharply with the study of the medium's interior world. Meanwhile in the U.S cities burned and students rioted. The new culture was aimed to "blow the mind" open rather than develop the mind's faculties. A psychedelic culture had arisen that was more concerned with challenging accepted standards of behaviour than examining man's psychic and spiritual nature. The new culture was hedonistic, ego-orientated and devoted to self-expression and fulfilment. The catalyst of the Vietnam War brought about a social revolution in the West. The World had turned and, on the face it, Mrs Miller's College had little in common wih 'Ziggy Star Dust and the Spiders from Mars'.

Robert Findlay at his Loch Lomond home, July 2007

There are now few at the College today who remember Major Robert Findlay, (not related to Arthur Findlay) a College Trustee, Treasurer and later Principal. He retired in 1979 and took up another post in the west of Scotland. The following extract from a memo illustrates that he had a certain mordant sense of humour. He here outlined the College's position for a meeting of the Council in March 1972.

A "Heriot Row is owned by the Trustees who hold it for behoof of the college or for any organisation having the same or similar objects...the choice resting with the Trustees. Thus the College is like a tenant on a repairing lease; they use and look after the building. They have been losing money gently for years and are now at the bottom of the barrel; there must be a change."

Findlay was saying that the Trustees were not bound to the College and could sub-let to any group who had similar objectives and a list was produced, which included, a yoga class, a Sufi study group, a Teilhard de Chardin Centre, healing, and meditation groups.

What was to be done? At a General Meeting of the members, on the 3rd of March 1972, chaired by Mr Findlay, the following situation was outlined (Findlay quotes 80/90 members for the year in question). The building was in serious need of repair with suspected subsidence to the southwest part of the College. It was in need, throughout, of re-wiring, re-plumbing and extensive decorating. The furnishings had grown old. In addition the Mews House at the back of the garden had already been sold, blocking street access to a garden that would have provided adequate parking facilities. The foundation was insolvent. There were various proposals to the effect of limiting the use of the building, which was too large. Perhaps, using only the member's drawing room and boarding out the speakers with members, parts of the College would be unused, reducing the need for a housekeeper. Further, events could be organised to raise funds such as a Summer Fair in the garden. The College used only four rooms when the whole building consisted of six floors of rooms. The basement was sub-let and produced a rent from the White Eagle Lodge. The Trustees had approached the SNU Trust Fund to help with the costs of refurbishment, only to find that the Trust lent money only to churches that were in full associated status and not to a Kindred Body such as the College.

The Council "resolved" the following: -

"Unanimously, Mrs Cargill abstaining, the college finds itself unable to continue to look after 30 Heriot Row for the Trust, and is obliged to vacate its responsibilities as quickly as possible, because the building is too big and expensive for its requirements. It asks the Trust to re-house it in more modest accommodation as soon as possible. Moreover, the College, now being insolvent, it asks the Trust to clear its debts from the proceeds of the sale and to arrange an overdraft to enable the College to pay its debts".

By June of that year with no rescue in sight the Trustees placed adverts in 'The Scotsman', which had brought serious enquiries, at the asking price of £20,000. The next building would ideally have a shop front which would be used to attract the passer-by. Ideally the new premises would be equipped with a large hall and other meeting rooms and the location would be as central as possible. In the event of a sale; temporary arrangements would need to be put in place for routine meetings to be able to continue and it was emphasised that each group would have to pay its way as the College Council was in no position to subsidise any meetings. The following example was drawn up. "Thus if a hall costs £2 per hour, then a two hour meeting would have to raise £4".

The Trustees, Mr Findlay, Miss Honywill, Mr Heddle and Mr Gardner, delegated Miss Honywill and Mr Gardner to label all the movable property in the building and to show what was for sale and what was for storage and to make appropriate arrangements with a removal firm for the end of July 1972.

No. 2 Melville Street, the first floor apartment home of the College from January 1973, with the entrance on the corner of Queensferry.

The date for moving turned out to be optimistic. Various halls were looked at from the point of view of suitability and expense. If booked soon,one particular hall was available, for a Wednesday and Friday night at £2 for the evening. Suitable lodgings for the visiting speakers were also found, with the Council agreeing that £7 to £10 a week was fair recompense for the three or four nights stay and for the provision during the day of private sitting facilities. In comparison, close at hand in Broughton Street, a short walk from Heriot Row, there were 'bed-sits' to be had at the going rate of £3 per week. A skilled tradesman would have been earning an average wage of £25 per week.

A view along Melville Street towards the Cathedral,
July 2007

The Trustees and Council were, in the summer of 1972, facing what has been called "the ship wreck of old age". With dreams over and uncertain times ahead, with dissension and apathy among the supporters, some who couldn't agree and some who walked away. No wonder the tone in Findlay's notes is of crisis management. The question was, could the vision of the Trustees take the College forward or would the "Centre fail and the College fall?" During the "interregnum", as Findlay came to call the transition to the new home, the disruption would have to be put up with; make do would be the order of the day, individual groups would have to shift for themselves and activities, if necessary, curtailed. The details of the sale and move may seem dry, yet there are often hints of the depth of emotion felt by some and the sorrow felt by others at the trauma taking place in Heriot Row. An appeal on behalf of Miss Honywill for assistance with ideas and practical suggestions fell on deaf ears, leaving "arrangements for private sittings, and the Wednesday and Friday groups members to look after themselves, if possible". By mid-June of that year the College was reporting a deficit of £500 and an outstanding loan of £250, or put another way, seven and half months' wages for a workingman.

There was a more daring plan and that was the proposed adaptation of 30 Heriot Row into flats. On the face of it, it is hard to see why the College Council did not take up the following idea. In April 1972, the Income Tax Office had confirmed that, in its view of the College's charitable status, there would be no tax payable on the letting of flats in 30 Heriot Row. Likewise the sub-letting of parts of Heriot Row to other organisations would, likewise, "not be assessable to tax". The Council sought professional advice from Henry Wylie and Partners, who in a letter confirmed that the £3,000 estimated by the Council for the conversion to flats was likely to be closer to £4,000. Wylie and Partners must have also been estate agents and surveyors for they ventured the opinion that there may be subsidence to the building and that the attic flat would need the installation of dormer windows to meet regulations for residence.

In addition, it was noted that an unusual grant was available up to June of 1973 for "doing up" flats for residence. £1,800 per flat was available to a total value of 75% of the cost of conversion. The following calculation gives a good impression of the size of Heriot Row, "Two flats out of the basement, one out of the ground floor and one out of the attic". That would leave the College "with lecture hall and the bedroom storeys for working areas for the College and other uses". It was thought that it may be difficult to get planning permission for change of usage to residential and/or commercial usage.

The sums look good. The grant would have produced £5,400 and the College would have had to find £3,600 to be repaid at 8 %, including base rate at 5% over ten years. Rents per flat per year would have been in the region of £900 for an unfurnished flat and £1,200 for a furnished flat, (From my personal memory, a three-bedroom house in North London at that time would rent at £2,400 per annum.) and that income would have been tax-free. You will remember in chapter one we said that a flat in Heriot Row today is available at £3,250 per month.

However, there the scheme faltered. Why cannot be definitely ascertained. The College was insolvent and in debt. The loans outstanding were with named individuals, many on the Council. Planning permission was said to be "difficult". The Trustees would have had to raise a loan of £3,600 to finance the conversions. There were many other problems with the building. Perhaps the whole plan was too complex and speculative? The current Principal Magnus McInnes commented that "...there just didn't seem any potential in flats in those days". In a letter to the Edinburgh College Council in 1974 Findlay stated that Heriot Row had been sold as it seemed "more practical than letting flats in Heriot Row...as it gives us some elbow room of income with which to make the College

Entrance to the new home of the College as it is today, July 2007

more effective". Perhaps the alternatives were tempting; a new home, one of more suitable size, debts paid and money in the bank. A new beginning somewhere fresh, away from the old place.

In June of 1972, Mrs Cargill, a member of the Council, resigned in protest at the selling of Heriot Row. Mrs Cargill's resignation was noted with thanks and regret. Unfilled posts on the Council were to be left vacant, suggesting that more than one member upped and left and the position of Treasurer was vacant.

On 5th June 1972, the gavel hit the wood at the accepted price of £27,000. over the advertised price in The Scotsman on 1st of June 1972. Folklore has it that Heriot Row was "done up" by speculators and thereafter sold for a considerable profit. The last ever meeting of the members at Heriot Row took place on the 15th June 1972, with a total of 18 being present including the Council and the Trustees. Nevertheless, the sale was over and above board and on the last day of August that year, the College had packed up what it could pack, sold off at auction what it could not and closed the door.

"We packed all that could be packed in the van and that's a fact;
And we got inside all we could get inside;
Then we packed all we could pack on the tailboard at the back,
Till there wasn't any room for me to ride"

In the end it came to the physical labour of packing, lifting, carrying and making arrangements for storage to be found, not least for the large library. The old man of the song, in this case was Robert Findlay under the stewardship of whom the College found a new home, a new direction and a future that would go on fulfilling the brief outlined by Mrs Miller. Without further dalliance the Trustees, College Council, members and associates and of course the Library, left Heriot Row and became homeless for a while but £27,000 better off. It had been emotional but they found a new home and could face the future free of debt and burdens.

The Trustees met on 23rd November 1972 and apparently bought the new premises on the basis of 'permission applied for' for change of usage. The Council must have been confident of being able to change the usage. During the "interregnum" regular activities such as public demonstrations of mediumship had

AUTUMN PROGRAMME, 1972

Wednesday Demonstrations, 3 p.m. (Door opened at 2.30 p.m.)

August 23—Mrs Agnes Porter, Barrhead.
August 30—Mr George Evans, Cardiff.
September 6—Mrs Cecily Moore, Belfast.
September 13—Miss Lilian Ayres, Tynemouth.
September 20—Mrs C. Constable, Aberdeen.
September 27—Mrs N. Saunders, Edinburgh.
October 4—Mrs Lexie Findlater, Grangemouth.
October 11—Mrs N. Hewit, Edinburgh.
October 18—Mrs Ivy Gilhespie, Glasgow.
October 25—Miss Ray Howden, Isle of Man.
November 1—Mrs Mary Kidd, Cadam, Nr. Cumbernauld.
November 8—Mrs Cecily Moore, Belfast.
November 15—Mrs C. Moore.
November 22—Mrs Lexie Findlater.
November 29—Mrs Agnes Porter.
December 6—Mrs Lexie Findlater.
December 13—Mrs Ivy Gilhespie.
December 20—Mrs Mary Duffy, Edinburgh.

Friday Demonstrations, 7.30 p.m. (Door opened 7 p.m.)

1972	*Speaker*	*Medium*
August 25	Mrs Agnes Porter.	Mrs A. Porter.
September 1	Mr George Evans.	Mr George Evans.
September 8	Mr Bill Gardiner.	Mrs Cecily Moore.
September 15	Miss Lilian Ayres.	Miss L. Ayres.
September 22	Mr Clive Hollands.	Mrs C. Constable.
September 29	Mr A. Gardner.	Mrs N. Saunders.
October 6	Dr John Beloff.	Mrs Lexie Findlater.
October 13	Mrs N. Hewit.	Mrs N. Hewit.
October 20	A.G.M. (Members).	6.45 p.m.
October 20	Mr J. Gilhespie.	Mrs Ivy Gilhespie.
October 27	Miss Ray Howden.	Miss Ray Howden.
November 3	Mrs Mary Kidd.	Mrs M. Kidd.
November 10	Rev. Donald Mackay.	Mrs Cecily Moore.
Nov. *17	Mr Alex. Gardner.	Mrs C. Moore.
Nov. *24	Mrs F. C. Whitson.	Mrs Lexie Findlater.
December 1	Mrs Agnes Porter.	Mrs A. Porter.
December 8	Mr Bill Gardiner.	Mrs L. Findlater.
December 15	Intimated later.	Mrs Ivy Gilhespie.
December 22	Mrs Mary Duffy.	Mrs M. Duffy.

(The College reopens on 5th or 10th January, 1973.)

*N.B.—Please note change in address of hall for meetings on 17th and 24th November, 1972.

(See announcements in Saturday's "Evening News.")

Programme for the Season that the College was without 'fixed abode'

continued at the BLESMA Hall, 24 Dundas Street that could only seat 50 people. (The hall was sub-let from the British Limbless ex-Service Men's Association aka BLESMA). Private sittings had been held at Miss Honywill's, though the lady had asked for six months release from secretarial work and presumably had forgone that part of her honorarium of £104 per year. In November, as the Trustees met the following figures were recorded:- the 82 members and 7 associates were paying £3.60 per annum in fees.

Then on 31st January 1973 they were able to move into their new premises at 2, Melville Street, off Queensferry, in the west end of the city. It was an apartment on the grand scale. The year after moving into the new home, College records note that membership was 71. The figures for membership appear to be estimates. Nowadays the figure is closer to 400 members. A new Council was quickly formed and people were co-opted from different groups such as healing, to make up the new body. Heaters were purchased, accommodation for the visiting speakers arranged within the apartment and as a resident caretaker was thought un-necessary for the smaller premises the post was therefore abolished. Planning permission was granted verbally by the city council but was not pursued, as part of the apartment would continue to be used as a bedroom and the premises could still be regarded as a private residence.

The fine library is rehoused in Melville Street . (Photograph July 2007)

The Council formally approved the new premises on the 2nd February 1973 and in that month Robert Findlay took over as treasurer. The council had paid £11,600 for the College's new home and would be charged £90 per year by the Edinburgh City Council for rates. An interesting change that took place that autumn was the abolition of the Board of Trustees. The old system of a College Council and a Trusteeship to manage the affairs of the property now appeared to be cumbersome and it was felt that here was an extra tier of bureaucracy that could well be done away with. This was agreed upon on the 2nd November 1973. The title deeds to all property being formally passed to the Edinburgh Psychic College and Library and the first general meeting of the members took place on the same day.

Major Robert Findlay became the first actual 'Principal' (1973-1979) and continued as Treasurer, that post to be held for one year. All preceding 'Principals' had been known as 'Honorary Principal'. Mrs Betty Smith became librarian with Brenda Laing as secretary. On the 8th of November that year the Council also decided to put to the members a suggested change of name to that of "The Edinburgh College of Parapsychology". The new title was thought to be more modern and scientific sounding. It had been used as the name of a foundation in Canada and later, (in 1984), there would be

Right:- Mrs Brenda Laing the College secretary at her desk in the late 1970s

Left:- William Saunders, Principal from 1979 to 1985, with Librarian Betty Smith at the Golden Jubilee Celebrations in September 1982.

a chair in Parapsychology endowed by Arthur and Cynthia Keostler at Edinburgh University.

At the AGM in 1973, a future Principal, William Saunders, (1979-1985) was nominated from the floor to be advanced "to the council" and "in case of any doubt agreed that he be appointed also an advisory-member from the 2.11.73". It was noted also that "nominations in future - 21days notice". There is a suggestion here that members wanted to introduce new people on to the Council. Further decisions that year involved the abolition of the associate member status.

One month later William Saunders, who is fondly remembered, found a role within the Council with Findlay, when the two formed a sub-committee known as the "Capital Finance Committee" to manage the College's Capital investments. They were empowered to "safe guard" the capital without reference to the rest of the Committee. In December of that year, The National Federation of Spiritual Healers (NFSH) was given "for insurance purposes" the task of running the College's healing facility with a College member, Mrs Currie, becoming an NFSH member.

Early in January 1974, Miss Honywill, a Trustee from Heriot Row days and a Council member issued a circular regarding the proposed change of name. It is not known what this circular contained; it may be assumed that Miss Honywill was opposed to changing the name of the College. In the same month the College itself produced a detailed outline of the implications of the name change. Unfortunately neither document has survived. On 1st March that year, a meeting of 20 members and 9 Council members voted 19 to 10 in favour of the change of name to the Edinburgh College of Parapsychology. Later that year Miss Honywill, who had been said to be "under strain", had resigned. The minutes of the AGM for 1973 made the following comment on Miss Honywill's service to the College:-

"No one could ever find the words sufficient to express the gratitude owed by the college to Miss Honywill. He did not know (the chairman, Mr Findlay) how many years she had been secretary but previous years must pale in to insignificance besides the difficulties of the last two, in which she had taken us out of Heriot Row, through the homeless wilderness and now safely in to port here, where we could comfortably set up shop. We know how close to her heart was the college's future and welfare......the burdens of which she had cheerfully borne for so long".

In 1974, in an effort to record the beginnings of the College, Findlay wrote to Catherine Mowat, who had been secretary to Mrs Miller for many years, for information on the early days of the College and memories of her employer. It is interesting to note Findlay's comment in the brief history written in 1974 and issued in the College's Golden Jubilee year that, had he known of the emphasis which Mrs Miller placed on the value of a good Library, he might have fought harder to retain the word Library in the new name. I assume that some of the copious notes left behind in the College archives are part of that project. The resulting leaflet (shown here) is still available today.

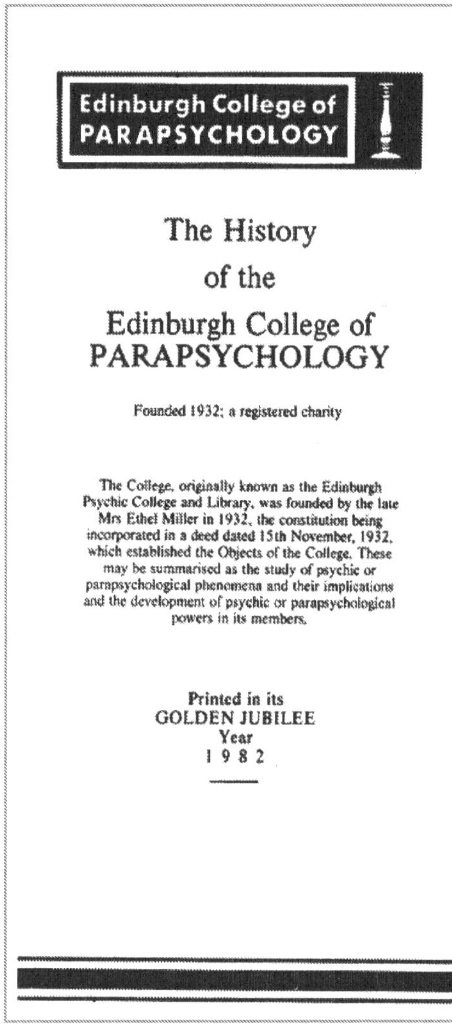

Edinburgh College of PARAPSYCHOLOGY

The History of the Edinburgh College of PARAPSYCHOLOGY

Founded 1932; a registered charity

The College, originally known as the Edinburgh Psychic College and Library, was founded by the late Mrs Ethel Miller in 1932, the constitution being incorporated in a deed dated 15th November, 1932, which established the Objects of the College. These may be summarised as the study of psychic or parapsychological phenomena and their implications and the development of psychic or parapsychological powers in its members.

Printed in its GOLDEN JUBILEE Year 1982

A trifold leaflet issued in celebration of the 50 years of the College

Although decimalisation had occurred in 1971, in February 1974, the notes still show fees paid in pounds, shillings and pence; a medium would be paid 80/- (£4) for private sittings at forty minutes and a guinea for platform work rising to £1.58 if a talk were also given. In October of that year, the newly reformed and renamed College also recorded its first deficit of £315, which was to be covered from the investments. The College did remain solvent and keeping an eye on the accounts was a principle concern of the College Council throughout the 1970's. Membership in 1979 rose to 160 at a fee of £5 per year; activities increased and the life of the College was resumed with renewed vigour.

The College was to enter a new era when Mr Robert Findlay indicated in May 1979 that he wished to resign from his posts and hand over to Mr Bill Saunders. Back in 1974, the Council had received confirmation from the College solicitors, Dundas and Wilson, that the Council could appoint to its board whomsoever they wished. Mr Saunders was unanimously elected as Principal and a Mr Alec Gardner was co-opted to be treasurer. Mr Findlay's letter of resignation made the following comments "I have been appointed Chairman of the Glasgow Branch of the Churches Fellowship for Psychical and Spiritual Studies". He went on to say:-

I have "resigned as treasurer of the College with an easy mind for two reasons. Firstly it is in a sound state, and there are no problems either current or on the horizon. We have come a long way since that chilly winter day when we first set foot in Melville Street, bringing with us a four figure loss and a commitment to a considerable revenue outlays on the new property. Not only is our financial position immeasurably stronger, but there is considerably greater activity in all our departments of our affairs". He spoke of Saunders and Gardner as having "long experience in our subject" and "are zealous for the College's welfare. Both are capable in business matters and sympathetic and harmonious in manner". He went on to thank Betty Smith, the librarian and Brenda Laing who had "taken the Lion's share of work as secretary when we have been in joint harness". His last words to the College were "...there is no reward in this work save in your gratitude and in the satisfaction in helping to contribute to the College's speciality and to our society and times".

Bill Saunders took over the helm as Principal in Spring 1979 and took the College forward. From this date until the launch of the Candlestick magazine in November 1998, there is little in the way of records of the College's activities but we do know of many of the mediums who served the College during this time (see Appendix). As Findlay had said the number and range of activities that the College provided had increased greatly. Melville Street was now also used as a meeting hall by many groups such as the Astrological study group, a Sai Baba study circle and the NFSH. These all helped to keep the College's doors open. The Lectures continued, a Sunday morning meditation meeting was convened "weather permitting"; regular Wednesday circles were on the programme and were well attended, as were the public demonstrations of mediumship and philosophy held on Fridays. In keeping with tradition no divine service was offered. The Wednesday open circle was so large by 1985 that it had to be split into two, with one being "closed" and attended only by experienced sitters and regularly led by the well known mediums who served the College.The other circle had a list of people who wanted to join.

One of the main events of this period was the celebration in 1982 of the 50th anniversary, chaired by Principal Bill Saunders and attended by, amongst others, future Principals Agnes Porter, Weilda White and the secretary Brenda Laing. It was agreed that

Golden Jubillee Celebrations:- Nita Saunders (left), Agnes Porter (Principal 1985-88) (centre), Bill Saunders behind right. The others are unknown.

Memories from the Golden Jubilee Celebrations, September 1982

LtoR:- Brenda Laing is seen here with Duncan Bickett, Chris Batchelor and Bill Saunders.

This happy group includes (from R) librarian Betty Smith, Weilda White (Principal 1988-96) and secretary Brenda Laing(3rd from right). The others are unnamed.

The audience included (L to R) College healer Elizabeth McLaren and Peggy Hood College Council member

More of the audience gathered to celebrate the occasion (including again, Elizabeth McLaren.)

the College would book the Guide Hall as the main hall at Melville Street can only seat 60 people and that Mary Duffy and Nita Saunders (who had served the College as a medium since at least 1972) would provide the demonstration. A speaker would also be booked. Mary Duffy appears not to have been able to attend so at a meeting in June 1982, the College council decided to approach Nita Hewitt and also Chris Batchelor with Nita Saunders. The event was a success and on that occasion wine was served.

While the College still had considerable investments, its day-to-day activities, for the year 1986, showed a deficit of £2,160. The shortfall may have been due to almost £2,350 having been spent on repairs and renewals. The only other figure available for this period, (1985), showed a smaller deficit of £1,299 and may also be related to repairs. However, the spectre of falling back in to debt must have been present in the mind of the Principal of the day.

Bill Saunders retired as Principal in 1985 and passed on the 3rd of December 1994. He had retired as a Chief Inspector of Police in the early to mid-1970's and had gone on to work as a case officer for the Edinburgh District Housing Department. His interest in Spiritualism led him to automatic writing and healing. His reputation has come down to us as a much liked and well trusted man. In 1985, around the same time as Bill Saunders' retirement, there was another change and Adeline Jack took over as Secretary for some years until the mid 1990s.

Agnes Porter took over as Principal until 1988. Angela McInnes says of this lady "Och, she was a lovely soul". Agnes had to withdraw for reasons of ill health and was succeeded by Weilda White (1988-1996). Weilda had by the mid-eighties given many years service on the College Council and also been Vice-Principal to Agnes Porter taking over from her when Agnes was no longer able to continue. It is remembered that along with her husband Douglas, the couple would regularly "do the shopping" for the College. Weilda is said to have held the College together through some difficult years, keeping the doors open, doing the work of the secretary and seeing the bookings were up to date as well as taking classes and working as a spiritual healer.

The well-loved visiting medium Albert Best with Mary Duffy. They shared a special friendship and frequently the platform at large demonstrations of mediumship. Both mediums travelled throughout the world working for Spirit. Albert was known to give communication from spirit in languages of which he hd no knowledge.(1)

In a ceremony unique in the history of the College on the 2nd June 1998 four members were made life honorary members. Adeline Jack, Nita Saunders, Mary Duffy and Weilda White were awarded gold life-time membership cards. In view of their long service and dedication to the College, the Council thought the distinction of honorary membership appropriate.

Ivor James, psychic Artist
1922-1998

In December of 1998 another good friend of the College, medium and psychic artist, Ivor James passed into spirit at the age of 76. His excellence and accuracy as a psychic artist is well remembered by Magnus MacInnes. On two consecutive visits to the College

Top left:- drawing by Ivor James, recognisd by Magnus as Ian McInnes, his brother, shown here in the family photo, on extreme right, behind.
Top right:- drawing by Ivor James, recognisd as Margaret McInnes by her son. Margaret is shown here in the famly photo (the lady, left front.).
(The drawings were done on white paper but because of the delicacy have been darkened to show the detail)

Ivor James executed two drawings which Magnus identified. The first, in 1991, was of his brother, Ian, and the following year he received one of his mother, Margaret McInnes.

Magnus Carnie Young McInnes, became Principal in 1996 and under him the College was to see a renaissance of activities. There was no background of Spiritualism in his family and it was in part the strain of a divorce and the work of bringing up two children by

Magnus McInnes, Principal of the College from 1996

himself that "chance" brought him into contact (during the course of his work) with a medium called Flannigan. Needless to say this meeting greatly changed him. He first came to the College in the early 1980s and it is recorded that he was re-elected to the Council in 1986. In his time the College has grown in membership and has been close to 400.

In 1976 Robert Findlay wrote this for the new College's newsletter: - "The College has a new format and name. The College is like a candlestick rather than the candle and it tries to arrange that a wide variety of candles have the opportunity to shine forth their light from it through the various activities and events and offerings which it tries to provide. Whether the light be from this side of life or the other, whether found in talks or books, in healing or in communication, giving to each his own chance to discover his stepping stones to progress in the infinite fields of Parapsychology".

The newsletter ran for several years but in November 1998 the new format came out in A5 size and 500 copies were distributed. Named 'The Candlestick', after Findlay's simile, it was issued to promote College services, advertise related subjects that may be of interest to the public and members and to keep members in touch with events in the College. The new journal was intended to be a quarterly. If you are a College regular you will be aware that the Principal always contributes a column "A message from the Principal". In the 2nd issue, April 1999, Magnus thanked the public for their support, praised the secretary, George Cornick, for his hard work in producing the magazine and informed the members that the 'Toilet' Appeal had been going well (presumably the appeal referred to the need to renew the facility). "The Fun Day" had been

The Candlestick

The Newsletter of the Edinburgh College of Parapsychology

ISSUE 7 November 2000

College Founder: Ethel Miller

Nita Saunders rededicates the memorial plaque to Mrs Miller
– see page 4

Christmas is for Children

... find out how you can help on page 4

Angela McInnes enjoys becoming an OSNU with her granddaughter
— fuller details on page 5

Linda Muir writes on Awareness in the Twenty First Century
(Pages 11-12)

a success and Angela McInnes was congratulated on gaining her CSNU and becoming an Assistant tutor at the Arthur Findlay College. The newsletter also announced a Private sitting would cost members £12 and non-members £14. Membership of the College was £15 or £12 to those in need of a concession.

Through these newsletters we know some eighteen mediums and speakers provided demonstrations of graphology and mediumship such as flower reading, transfiguration, trance and clairvoyance. In 1999, as the 20th century drew to a close the cost of attending these demonstrations was £3.50 to members and £4 for non-members.

In addition, some ten workshops were offered at costs between £15 and £23 according to the length of the workshops, some last two days. The new Principal saw affordability as being a key to the growth of the College.

History is not simply about the distant past. In recording details of very recent times this book "Mrs Miller's Gift" is seeking to record those details which are so often missing from archives and which will form the story of today in years to come. In addition I like to compare and contrast the current details with those of the past. It has come down to us as folklore that the College was regarded by some as being a 'little expensive' and therefore not as open and inclusive as it could have been. Magnus McInnes saw the way forward to be by making the College and its services more accessible and affordable. As any good leader should have, Magnus had a vision of how the College could move ahead in its brief of serving others.

Angela McInnes's associations with the College go back nearly thirty years. There was some interest in Spiritualism within her family through a relative who had connections to the Albany Street Spiritualist Church. Through the College, Angela had a private sitting which, like her husband, altered her life. Angela and Magnus were married at the registrar's office in 1987. Angela gradually became more involved with the activities of the College. She eventually joined the Council in the early 1990's and was the secretary for awhile. Through the SNU, Angela was awarded the Certificate of the Spiritualist National Union (CSNU) and in November of 2000, she became an Officiant (OSNU) and went on to be a fully accredited tutor at the Arthur Findlay College, Stansted.

Angela McInnes OSNU

In Scotland, Angela is

known as a "Celebrant" and is able to personally register a marriage, unlike in England, where an Officiant still needs a Registrar present to register a marriage. In the autumn of 2006, Angela celebrated the marriage of the then Treasurer and Healer Dr. Stephen Harding to Gloria Teven. Stephen's associations with the College go back several years and many know of his hard work. Stephen had been treasurer for 11 years and was a council member before that. He assisted with the setting up The Candlestick magazine in its new format and with the installation of the computer systems. Security has been tightened in recent years with the introduction of CCTV to the entry hall. Dr Harding who though not a medical doctor has also acted as Healing Leader. In recent years his practical and financial help have been invaluable. With Stephen, George, the secretary and Magnus, have developed catering skills and the trio have fed many mouths at weekend work-shops and summer schools.

Stephen Harding and Gloria Teven are married ... *see page 5*

The marriage, as illustrated in The Candlestick Autumn 2006, with Angela McInnes as Celebrant.

Since the changes of the 1990s, the College has had a vigorous resurgence in activities and it is fair to say that it has flourished and matched the early years of its history. In the summer of 2000, the College entered the technological era with the launch of its own web-site www.parapsychology.org.uk and its own email address, secretary@parapsychology.org.uk. Also, that year the college took an interest in the charitable work of the "Children 1st" and raised £1,100 but it was in the core area of the College's activities that the College saw the greatest increase. Other facilities, such as the library and the College shop have grown appreciably in recent years. The library continues to rely upon the donations and support of the members and has developed in to one of the largest and oldest such collections in the United Kingdom, with new books and new topics being added all the time.

Stewart Alexander

Raymond Smith

Colin Fry on stage at Portobello Town Hall, Edinburgh in 2003

In March of 2000, the physical, trance and clairvoyant medium Colin Fry[(2)] first visited the College to give private sittings and demonstrations. Colin demonstrated trance with his guide Magnus giving a talk and then engaging the audience in a question and answer session. Colin returned twice in 2003 and on one occasion gave a public demonstration of clairvoyance for the College in Portobello Town Hall to 600 people, with many being said to be new to "Spiritualist" demonstrations and another at the Church Hill Theatre. In this both Colin and the College were carrying on an old tradition which started with Helen Hughes, Maurice Barbanell and Hannen Swaffer.

Other traditions continue to be honoured. Raymond Smith of Gibraltar has visited to give trance discourses by well known figures from the Spiritualist and Psychical Research movement of years ago, such as Oliver Lodge.[3]

In the tradition of Helen Duncan, Stewart Alexander came to the College in May of 2005. As many physical mediums of the past had done, Stewart gave a physical séance, a trance demonstration and a lecture. Members of his circle, June and Alf Winchester were on hand with their support. The medium delivered one of his well-received talks on "Rods, and Pods and Alchemy" which illustrated the lives of the physical mediums of the past. That evening Stewart gave a deep trance demonstration and many evidential messages were accepted by the audience.

This is what the report of the sitting in Psychic World had to say of the following day:-

"On the Sunday, in the library "sanctum", with blackout complete, during a two hour séance the sitters witnessed the 'passage of matter through matter'. The departed Dr Barnett[4] made a spirit return and gave Mary Armour healing. Mary herself has served the College many times. Ectoplasmic hands were seen in red light and the light metal 'trumpets' were seen to dance in the air. Stewart's regular communicators, Freda Johnson and Walter Stinson (who died in 1911, in a railway accident) both chatted with the visitors at the séance; much the same as Laura Culme Seymour had experienced at the College 70 years earlier. At the end of the sitting, Stewart's main guide, White Feather spoke, closing the evening with a blessing."

I am reminded of what Laura had to say of such occasions "...indeed it is a never to be forgotten experience and my heart is full of gratitude to the almighty God for all that I have been allowed to see and hear".

The teaching role of the College has gathered apace in recent decades, with core activities such as awareness classes, open and closed circles, meditation classes, Spring and Summer schools, all readily available. The object is to meet the College's core purpose of taking the student to further stages of excellence in standards of mediumship development. In addition and independently, recently

The lounge showing the windows which look down onto Queensferry. The bronze bust of Helen Duncan can be seen in the corner and a photograph of Mrs Allan hangs on the wall.

one autumn some eleven "workshops" were being offered. These cover all manner of topics and are provided externally by people who use the College facilities.

The present secretary George Cornick became involved in the College through his contact with Angela and Magnus McInnes who were his next door neighbours. Angela had known George since school days. There was no history of things psychic in his family but through his neighbours he found himself drawn in to the life of the College. In particular George brings a business background to his role at the College. He became Secretary having been involved with the College since the mid-1990s. As well as producing The Candlestick magazine regularly, many of the technological innovations have been introduced by George. The role of secretary

One distinguished speaker at the College has been Psychic Researcher Prof. Archie Roy. With more than 50 years of investigation behind him he has a wealth of information to impart. He once described his life as being like a "Dr Jekyll and Mr Hyde existence. By day a respectable astronomer, by night the parapsychologist and psychical researcher. It is a double life which certainly has been fruitful."(5)

has always been very important in the life of the College and often it is they who have kept the bookings moving along and feet coming through the door.

With the launch of digital television channels and programmes about mediumship in the early 21st century the College found its self well positioned to benefit from the increased interest shown by the public in demonstrations of mediumship. The Spiritualism that was commitment free and that was represented by the College found a ready response with a public which was looking for an organisation that met their needs without requiring a commitment in return. This is the essence of their 'Customer Service'. Further, the College, via its web-site, email and data-base, had developed tools of focusing the requirements of the potential public through advertising the services that were on offer. Customer service and focus are the modern tools of a service business. By matching service and focus with high standards of mediumship at affordable prices the Edinburgh College of Parapsychology had hit upon a modern formula to match an old agenda.

5 "...Among my souvenirs ...."

Every man has two Educations: -
the one he is given and the one he gives himself.
Tynman

Essential to Mrs Miller's vision for the College and as a resource for the student to search for answers, was a library. This has over the years accumulated souvenirs of experiences and research within its walls. Books, artefacts, photographs, ephemera and other records have found a home here. Some of the pieces which have found their way into the College are not so ephemeral either, for the College's associations with physical mediumship go back even further than its own foundation, and the presence of Helen Duncan within its walls, to Daniel Dunglas Home (1833 -1886).

Home, born near Edinburgh in 1833 but taken, as a child, to live in America, was a renowned physical medium on both sides of the Atlantic and in Europe, frequently demonstrating his remarkable power for the aristocracy and wealthy but never accepting any money for his demonstrations. The following, amazing levitation took place when Home was only 19, in the Connecticut home of Mr Ward Cheney, a wealthy businessman, in front of a Mr F. L. Burr, whose assignment it was to find some incriminating evidence, against Spiritualism in general, and especially about Home, who had his debunkers in an uproar with his excellent reputation. However, instead of writing an expose of the

evening, Burr instead wrote: "Suddenly, without any expectation on the part of the company, Home was taken up into the air. I had hold of his hand at the time and I felt his feet - they were lifted a foot from the floor. He palpitated from head to foot with the contending emotions of joy and fear which choked his utterances. Again and again he was taken from the floor, and the third time he was taken to the ceiling of the apartment, with which his hands and feet came into gentle contact."(1)

The D.D. Home Drinking Fountain in its prime when it stood in Canongate.

On July 3rd 1888, Edinburgh town Council gave permission for a memorial to be erected opposite the Canongate Church by Mrs Home, in memory of her husband, at the considerable cost of £400.

By 1951, the Clerk of Works for Edinburgh said the memorial was in need of much repair, as the stonework was loose and it

The pile of rubble which had been D.D. Home's memorial, 1959

should be removed. It was pulled down and the pile of rubble remained for some years in the yard of Scott & Brown, Builders.

Late in1959, the College Council rescued the inscription stone from that drinking fountain. It now has a place at the Edinburgh College and was unveiled in February 1960.

The fireplace in the lounge of the College with the D.D.Home Memorial stone on the Hearth and a fine portrait of Thomas Miller above it.

Another unusual feature owned by the College is a large symbolist painting. On 16th June 1938, the College staged an exhibition of symbolic and decorative paintings by the french ex-miner, Augustine Lesage. Each work was completed while Lesage was in trance, under the control of his guides, and knew nothing of what had occurred. He was apparently uneducated and quite without artistic training. Some 450 large-scale canvases were produced in this manner. Much of the work was delicate and required precision of application. Yet the former miner felt no fatigue and worked for hours under spirit control.

Mrs Miller was 'taken by the "designs" and bought several', one of which is still to be seen in the College.

Augustine Lesage with Mrs Miller(right) and Mrs Allan (left) and an unknown lady at the exhibition of his work in the College, June 16th 1938.

A souvenir postcard showing M. Lesage with one of his symbolist paintings

Above:- M· Augustine Lesage - dressed as the miner he was, on one of his souvenir publicity postcards sold at the exhibition and signed on the reverse, as shown below.

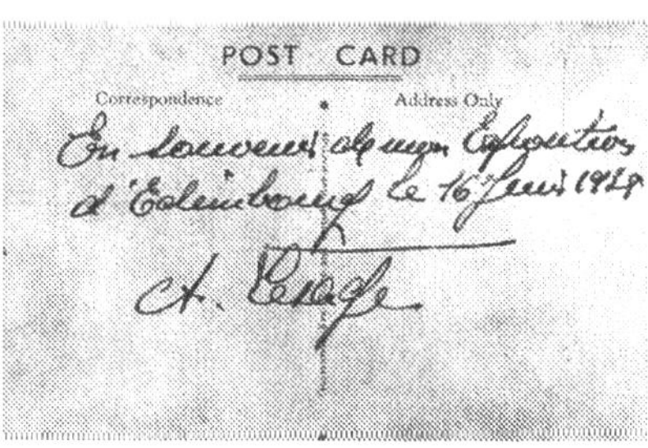

SYMBOLIC PICTURES

French Ex-Miner's Work

THERE has been placed on exhibition at Edinburgh Psychic College during yesterday and to-day a collection of symbolic and decorative designs in colour by M. Augustin Lesage, a French ex-miner, who paints under "control." The impetus to paint, he states, came to him suddenly, and he commenced the first elaborate design on a canvas measuring about 9 feet square without previous training. Some of the large decorative designs have been exhibited in the Salon des Artistes and the Salon d'Automne, Paris. In the latter was shown "L'Esprit de la Pyramide" in 1928. "Composition symbolique sur le monde spirituel" was hung in the former in 1932. The most impressive feature of the early and later works is the minuteness of the detail and the manner in which small decorative devices and arrangements are repeated with machine-like exactness. In the later works there is a notable symmetry and balance. At first one has the impression that this is a matter of duplication in reverse, but examination reveals a remarkable variety of detail. In some, Egyptian figures and symbols are introduced; there are also Hebraic and Assyrian motives and devices. One of the designs has been acquired by Mrs Miller, founder of the College, to be hung there permanently. It is largely Egyptian in character.

The artist's "controlled" method of painting, akin to the manner of automatic writing, has been examined and vouched for by the Institut Metapsychique of Paris, under the direction of Dr Osty.

An address on M. Lesage's painting under control was given in the College last night by Mrs Helene Fry, of London, who is interpreter for M. Lesage during his tour. She mentioned that he had painted some 450 of these large designs with enormous multiplication of detail. It was difficult to understand how one whose hands had been hardened by toil had been able to execute work requiring such delicacy and skill, and having all the accuracy of a miniature. He never knew when he began what the work was going to be. There were introduced into the design fabulous fishes and birds and beasts, varied objects, houses, images, Chinese junks, and other vessels, and an endless variety of other motives. He worked quickly and without erasing, and while doing so was in a sort of semi-sleep. Some of the designs seemed to have a hidden meaning; they appeared to illustrate ceremonies of initiation.

A number of questions were put at the close of the address. In reply to one, M. Lesage said he had no conscious knowledge of the effects of mixing different colours. He knew instinctively what colours to select and mix.

A newspaper article reporting Lesage's presence in Edinburgh in June 1938, possibly written by the College's friend, journalist J.W. Herries.

One of the Augustine Lesage paintings purchased by Mrs Miller at the exhibition in 1938. It still hangs in the lecture room of the College but this reproduction does not do justice to the fine colouring.

In the lounge of the College at Melville Street are other art-works that belonged to the Miller family including, a fine portrait of Mr Miller senior, of whom she was very fond,(*see page 115*) and a Norwegian landscape with rustic house.

The College has, over the years, made a conscious effort at keeping the memory of Helen Duncan alive. In the Library was an over-looked detailed account of her mediumship in the form of Laura Culme-Seymour's book 'Marjorie', signed by the author. Also hidden away were three 78 rpm. records numbered 3a/b 4a/b and 5a/b. The first part of the sequence, 1 a/b and 2 a/b, is missing. The rather plain labels clearly indicate that they were live amateur recordings made at a séance possibly in the late 1930's. We were able to play them and hear again the voices of sitters at a Helen Duncan séance, silent for so many years. Maybe they were recorded at the College. Some characters among the sitters were known, one, a Mrs Roughhead of Belgrave Crescent, Dean Bridge, Edinburgh, hosted séances for Helen Duncan, which Laura Culme-Seymour attended. 'Albert', Helen Duncan's guide is addressed and he replies. Helen herself is referred to by one of the sitters.

A further set of 78 rpm. records was discovered. And from out of the long silence came Ernest Oaten's mellow tones from a 1934 BBC recording speaking about "What Spiritualism means to me". Discovering, that which has been overlooked is the joy of being a researcher. Further preservation work will be needed on these records but it is hoped that a CD can, in the near future, be produced from these recordings.

The college has on display a fine bust of Albert Stewart, Helen Duncan's guide. The piece is now displayed in the lounge of the College, but how it came to be in the College is unknown. A Psychic News article of the late 1930's, gives the following account of its origin. Mrs Mary Slater, a psychic artist of York and Mr F. W. George, a sculptor of Aberdeen, independently of one another, produced portraits of the famous guide. Both gave the same title to their work "A disciple" even though they were not in touch with each other. The guide had "sat" for both and offered criticism of the work in progress to both artists. Initially, Mrs Slater had drawn up images of Albert, placed them between two sheets of paper and when next at a séance had asked the guide for his comment. Albert replied, "Yes it's like me but I don't like the mouth it makes me look too stern". The abberation was corrected with Albert's help and Mrs Duncan gave Mrs Slater the address of the sculptor at Aberdeen.

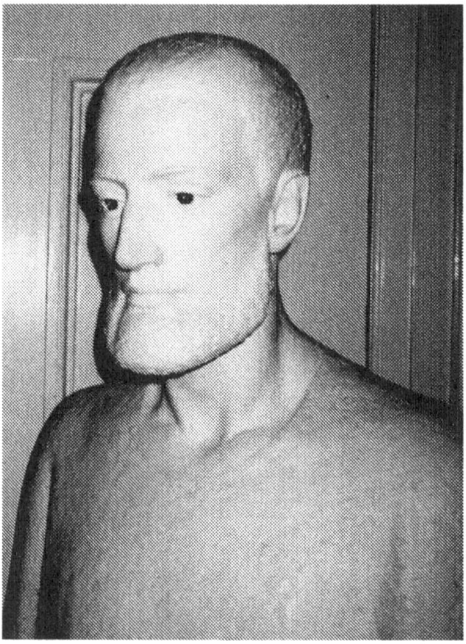

Bust of Helen Duncan's guide, Albert Stewart, sculpted by F.W. George of Aberdeen.

Mr George had said to his wife that he would have liked to model Albert but that he never showed his face. That evening at a séance Albert said "I received your thought." He then materialised and showed his face and beard. On receipt of Mrs Slater's letter and drawings he forwarded his drawings for the bust of Albert, to her. When the work was completed.Albert expressed his satisfaction During the séance that evening an idea came to Mr George regarding the name of the sculpture and Albert gave his approval at the choice of name, 'A Disciple' which had also been used by Mary Slater.

When Mrs Duncan was at York the guide said to Mrs Slater "I want you to have a good look at my features. She reports, "He then materialised and stood still. His face appeared to be lit with a bright interior light, which illumined every feature and glistened on his dark hair and curly beard. I could see the pupils of his large brown eyes". He then said to her, "You may worry yourself that the nose is too aquiline or too Jewish or any other shape, but I tell you that your sketch is very like me indeed."

The Slater family were prominent Spiritualists and Joseph Slater (1853-1902) was one of the founders of the York Spiritualist Church. His widow, attended many séances with Helen Duncan at Fountayne Street in York. Mrs Mary Slater would have been married into the Slater family of York, and it is possible that she was known also as Mrs Percy Slater shown in the photo, here, taken by Billy Hope in 1932. All the sitters in the photograph were known

to have sat with Helen Duncan and it is recorded that Helen Duncan visited York to give séances in 1938, which ties up with the newspaper article which is placed amongst some other College clippings for 1938 to 1939. It is reasonable to presume that the sculpture was produced along with the drawings in those two years and was displayed in the Scottish Academy in Edinburgh..

Women of the Slater family of York, in a 'spirit' photograph by Billy Hope in 1932.

Another tribute to Helen Duncan, on show in the lounge, was commissioned by the White Rose Fellowship and crafted by the artist, Mrs Maureen Mailley. This piece of artwork is cast in bronze and dates from 1996/ 1997.

It was first exhibited at Berkeley Street Church, in Glasgow where Helen Duncan gave many séances. It initially was intended to have the bust displayed in Helen Duncan's home town of Callander and then it was thought that the sculpture should go to Helen's family, but neither option came to pass and the bronze bust found an honoured home in the College in Melville Street.

Bronze bust of Helen Duncan now on display in the College lounge.

Amongst the more ephemeral and fragile of the souvenirs which have survived are the psychic photographs. Some of these may have been inherited from the societies which predated the foundation of the college. One we do know to have been taken by Robert Boursnell in the latter part of the 19th century.

The sitter, J.H.Evans, with an extra of a coloured child. Photo by R.Boursnell in 1895.

Other very old 'spirit photos' taken and shown on the next two pages, have survived in a small album at the College, which has the inscription on the flyleaf, "With kind remembrances from H. Blackwell" but with no other details about the photographs it holds, the sitter, or the photographer. We feel we may assume, from the date of the photos, that these are the work of Robert Boursnell. Mr H. Blackwell, a Vice President of the SSSP (Society for the Study of Supernormal Pictures)(2) in the early part of the 20th century, said of Boursnell's work, " In my many sittings with him, extending over a period of ten years.........Having made a close study of the subject....., aided by a very large collection of psychic photographs, and being an amateur photographer, I am fully convinced that Mr Boursnell is absolutely honourable and worthy of the utmost respect."(3) And Arthur Conan Doyle said of Blackwell "his experiences have been exceptional, he is one of the pioneers in the history of Psychic photography."(4)

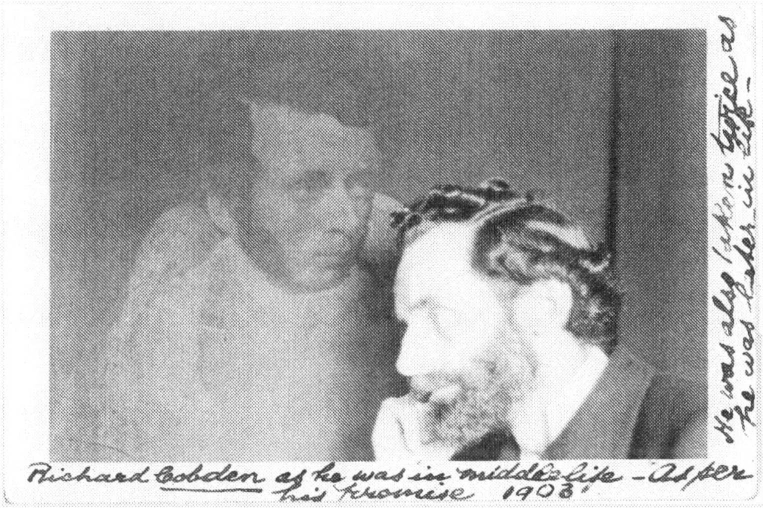

Spirit image of Richard Cobden probably taken by Robert Boursnell.

The sitter is the same in all of the pictures and he appears to attract well-known 'spirit extras'. Shown above is one with a spirit image of Richard Cobden. Cobden was a manufacturer and reformer who, in 1846, successfully campaigned against the Corn Laws. The legend around the picture tells us that the Spirit extra was, "as he was in middle life - as per his promise 1903. He was also taken twice as he was in later life." We have not found these other pictures.

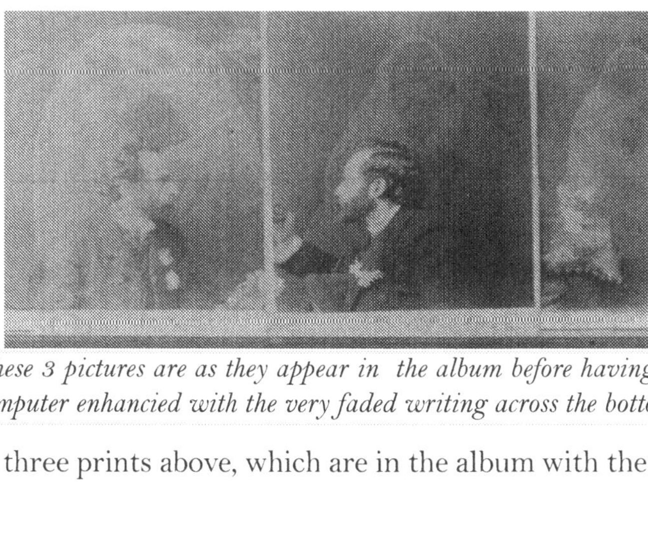

These 3 pictures are as they appear in the album before having been computer enhancied with the very faded writing across the bottom.

The three prints above, which are in the album with the Cobden print bear the legend that Charles Dickens, Thomas Carlyle and John Ruskin are the spirits who have shown themselves. The photographs and writing are faded now but with computer 'contrast' enhancement we have been able to read the inscription and know

L to R. 'Extras' are identified on the originals as Charles Dickens, Thomas Carlyle and John Ruskin

These two photos show the same sitter and are believed to be taken by Boursnell. In the picture on the left it is as though the face has not had the chance to form fully. In the right-hand picture the face and drapery are clearly defined. (The first picture has been given more contrast to show the face developing in the 'mist')

that they were taken in 1901. We hope that you can make out the faces and the comparisons in art-work done of them, during life.

Other photos in the archives include examples of Billy Hope's mediumship. The one shown below was recognised and has been reprinted with a photo showing the young man as he was in life. Unfortunately his name has nor been recorded but assume he was lost in World War I.

An Unknown Soldier as captured by Billy Hope (undated).

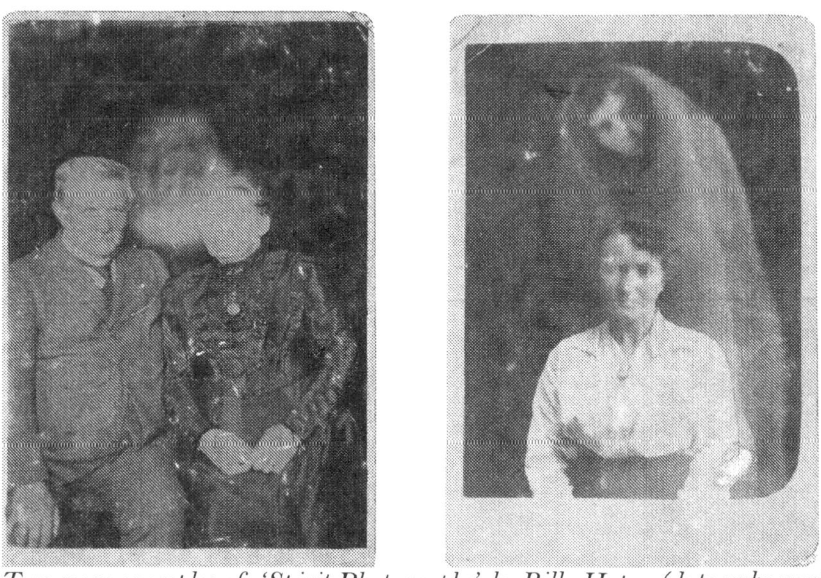

Two more examples of 'Spirit Photographs' by Billy Hope. (date unknown)
Left:- 'spirit extra' - Cathie Galloway. *Right:- Mrs McLenon*

The sitter in this picture recognised the 'spirit extra' as his mother, attributed to Billy Hope

Taken in H B Raines Circle showing Mrs M McKenzie with Mother and Father

The 'spirit extra' in this photograph was identified by her son, the sitter, as his mother and her memorial photograph has been attached alongside. (Computer contrast enhancement has been applied to help the reader make the comparison.)

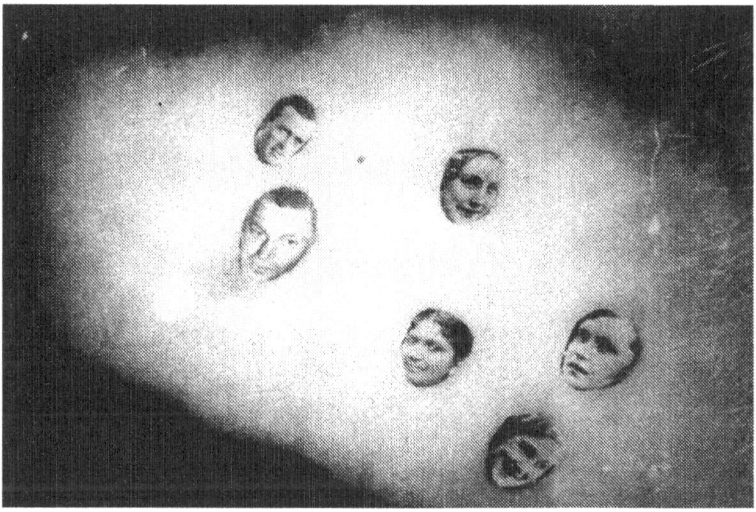

This style of 'spirit photography' was typical of the work of John Myers. This is thought to have been taken at the College

There are many other examples of 'Spirit' photographs in the archives and this could be a fruitful area of research for anyone interested in the subject but this final picture, although residing in a book in the college library, we know it was taken in London on the 8th April 1936 by the Falconer Brothers, with one of them sitting alongside Laura Culme Seymour when an 'extra' of her daughter Marjorie was obtained. Laura says that she saw the plate developed with a plainly visible 'extra' and a few days later received a print of it. Falconer said he had plainly seen the same form when Laura had first entered the room.[5]

Psychic photo of Marjorie taken by Mr Falconer, 8th April 1936.

Above:- Colin Evans, physical medium with a 'trumpet' floating in front of him. Photo by resarcher Nandor Fodor.

Right:- Colin Evans levitating over the hundreds of sitters at a mass meeting in the Conway Hall, CamdenTown,London in 1938.

Very little is known of the mediumship of Colin Evans but this series of five photographs appeared in an article written by him in the magazine 'Photography' in January 1939. Research has shown that the photograph of Evans levitating was taken at the Conway Hall, in Camden Town in 1938 in front of 600 hundred people. The photograph is said to have been taken by a Press photographer from the Daily Mirror which devoted a whole page to the photgraph and the eyewitness report by the photographer.

Ectoplasm streaming from the nostril of Colin Evans at another mass meeting. Photo believed to be by Léon Isaacs.

luminous tape on Evans' hands and feet enabled the audience to follow him as he floated over their heads in the hall which was in total darkness. He remained in the air continuously for about one minute at an average height of 15 feet above the ground. As the infra-red flash destroyed the power holding him up the photograph was taken at a point when the fall would not injure anyone in the audience[(6)]. These photographs were all taken by infra-red flash in total darkness.

Evans was a University graduate and worked professionally in literary work, describing himself as a 'spare time' medium. His mediumship had developed in the early 1930s after he had been trying to hoax a friend. In his own words :-

"I was in those days a complete and completely ignorant unbeliever and mocker, and, feeling bored and a little contemptuous one night in the company of an acquaintance who was a convinced

Spiritualist, when the talk turned on automatic writing I tried, by way of a jocular "leg pull," to test the credulity of a Spiritualist by pretending to get automatic writing myself. And while I was toying with a pencil, trying to think of something to write, and unaware that I was writing anything, his exclamation drew my eyes to two lines of mirror-writing (which I could not have done normally to save my life, never having practised or attempted it) that my hand had written at lightning speed, which read: "If Colin would stop fooling and take this seriously he would be very useful to us."(7) According to the article in Photography, he was well known in the Spiritualist movement as a speaker and a writer as well as a medium but at this distance in time we have been unable to discover more about him and are grateful to the College archive that this has come to light.

Many physical mediums followed the custom of holding Christmas Tree parties for Spirit children when small toys would be placed on or around the tree for the children to play with during the séance(8). In some Home Circles, the toys had disappeared from the room by the end of the sitting(9). The two

Above:- Before the Colin Evans' Christmas Tree sitting.
Right:- During the Colin Evans' Christmas Tree sitting.
Photos by Léon Issacs at Evans' own home.

photographs shown here illustrate a Christmas Party Séance in the home of Colin Evans - before and during the sitting. Notice the scattered disturbance of the toys etc around the base of the Christmas tree in the picture on the right. The photos were taken in Evans' own home with 20 invited guests "on the birthday of a little boy whose birthday had been near Christmas. The tree was 4 feet high and embedded in earth in a heavy wooden box. Between the two photos being taken the tree was thrown about by the spirits and the toys left scattered all over the floor."(10)

Evans' mediumship had been the subject of close investigation by Dr Nandor Fodor who was an early visitor to the College, as we have seen from the Visitor's Book entry on page 47. Dr Fodor, as a psychical researcher, may also have attended some of the Colin Evans séances illustrated on these pages. He certainly took infra-red photographs of him levitating. Born in Hungary in 1895, Fodor studied Law before coming to England to work as a journalist for Lord Northcliffe and developed a deep interest in both psychical research and psychoanalysis. He was appointed Research Officer for the International Institute for Psychical Research and compiled his well-known 'Encyclopedia of Psychic Science' in 1934. This book is still considered one of the best available on the subject, though the new edition combines it with a similar work by Lewis Spence.(11)

Moving back to our less ephemeral artefacts, the turn of the Millenium saw the plaque commemorating Mrs Miller's passing, in 1946, re - dedicated by Nita Saunders, a life long working member of the college. The report of the occasion was featured in 'The Candlestick' newsletter in November 2000.

The small portrait of Mrs Miller, which is shown in detail at the front of this book, hangs above the plaque commemorating her life.

Following the move, continuity was seen, by many of the older members of the college, to be keeping everything, as near as possible, as how it had been in Heriot Row. Besides the paintings which Mrs Miller had left, as her legacy, there were also two tapestries. They still hang in the college but nothing is known of their origin except that they appear to be Chinese. The Millers did travel widely and perhaps they were a souvenir of a memorable trip.

The rear of the Lecture Room showing the Lesage picture on the left and the one of the tapestries left as a legacy by Mrs Miller.

In the 1970s many of the woven wicker chairs, which had been in the lounge at Heriot Row were still in good condition and continued to be used but by the 1990s the joints were becoming loose. In an age of personal tape recorders, this led to complaints to the management that the squeaks and creaks of the old furniture were obscuring the details of communications during sittings. Finally, during the time of Weilda and Magnus, a change had to be made and new furniture was acquired.

Amongst other pieces which date back to the founding of the College in 1932 is a print of a picture of Jesus. In 1974, Robert Findlay commented on this picture in his introduction to the brief history. He wondered, 'What was the story behind that picture?' He was referring to a print of a painting, the original of which is 10 feet high and has place of honour in a private chapel in Stockholm. It had been painted directly from a vision of the Christ by the Swedish artist Bertha Valerins.

Keiko Mukaide's work in place in the Lecture room at the College

As the College has a non-religious foundation, many felt that it may give an impression that the College had, in effect, a Christian bias, especially as the picture was hanging on the wall at the back of the dais in the lecture room, where mediums give demonstrations of their mediumship. The Council decided in 2003 to replace this print with a new piece of Art and approached one of their own members, artist Keiko Mukaide, to produce for them a work to her own design which would be full of colour but have no obvious connotation .

Keiko Mukaide

Keiko was born in Japan in 1954. She studied in Tokyo, USA, London and Europe before, in 1993, coming to Edinburgh College of Art, first as an 'Artist in Residence' then from 1999 to the present day as a 'Research Fellow'. She has won a number of Scottish Arts Council Awards as well as Awards from other bodies. Since 2001 she has carried out a number of commisssions for Public

Buildings throughout Scotland and the North of England; buildings as diverse as Galleries, a Cinema and a hospital, working mainly in glass and glass tiles. An active member of the Awareness group and meditation group, Keiko occasionally uses her artistic skills, combining many different materials for meditations or energy work, whether in the college itself or, once, in the Palm House in the Botanic Gardens.

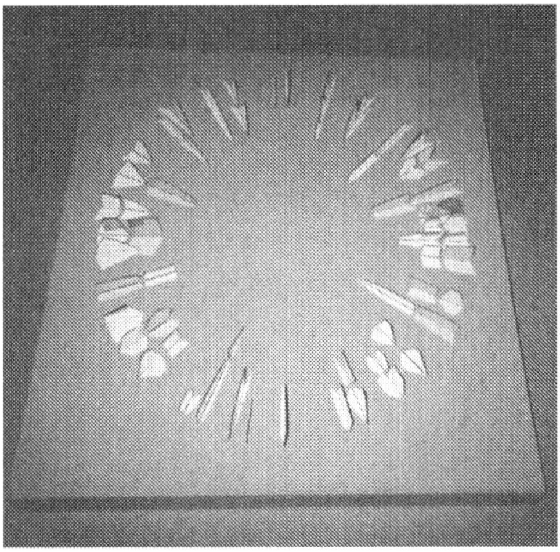

A closer view of the Art Work by Keiko

The delicate collage, made in coloured glass of the quality used in photographic filters, cannot be shown at its best in black and white so we decided to place a picture of it on the back cover of this book, where it can be in colour. But, of course, the best place to see it is in the College itself.

The cost of such a piece was a little daunting for the College but the artist waived half her fee and most of the rest of the money came from two very generous donations to enable another memorable piece to be added to the Treasure House which is the Edinburgh College of Parapsychology.

6 *"... water-colour memories of the way we were."*

A Personal Memory by Nita Saunders

On being asked to write an article for this publication in celebration of 75 years, it was difficult to know just where to start, causing me many hours of contemplation, and searching of memory. Memories which would fill a hundred volumes!

I do not doubt that many words will be written and spoken at this time, and I often feel sad that so often it is the names of long deceased and oft forgotten celebrities that are the greatest memories and of course they should not be forgotten, those trailblazers who were mainly responsible for where we are today. But they truly were so often just the icing on the cake.

I have known Spirit all my life, having been brought up in a family where the presence of Spirit was an accepted part of our life. My father, who was a much respected architect in Edinburgh, and my mother a housewife - (as most women were in those days), were among the founder members of The Psychic College and Library in 1932. The frequent visits to The College meant that it was an accepted source of conversation in our home and on becoming a schoolgirl at, what was then, The Edinburgh Ladies College in Queen Street, it was very common for me to go to Heriot Row and meet my mother after school on a Wednesday afternoon, when she would be amongst the group of helpers who were always there. In retrospect I realise how very fortunate I was to have met and talked with so many of the now legendary names of mediumship. I was also permitted to see and often take part in the various 'projects' that were going on, and I believe that I have witnessed - if not every - certainly 99% of all types of Spiritual communication and psychic phenomena, presumably because Spirit knew where my life would lead and deemed it necessary for me to partake of such experiences - none of which I have forgotten, the young mind retains such information. It was The College which was to become my Alma Mater, and start me on a journey through life which was undoubtedly predestined.

However, I am just one of the thousands and thousands of folk who have benefited from the ministrations of The College and the folk who have passed through its doors. Many souls have received solace, knowledge and comfort over its lifetime, not only from the various mediums who have worked there, but from the friends and workers, the visitors and guests, the council members and the countless volunteers who were happy to give of their time freely in their quest to help others. Those souls were and still are vital to the continuation of The College, the true workers for Spirit., without them the mediums would have nowhere to work, the bereaved and desperate nowhere to come and The College would - quite simply - not exist!

I have very clear memories of some of them; how many of us I wonder remember the late Nan Mitchell, with her pawky sense of humour, informing us in her quiet and dignified way that she was in training to become the next Chancellor of the Exchequer as she wandered round the lounge collecting the tea money! However, I will ever hold in awe the late Miss Mae Inglis who for a long period of time round about the 50s to 70s, I suppose, did just about everything at Heriot Row. She was a small slightly built lady with an unfortunate hare-lip and cleft palate which could make her speech difficult to understand sometimes, but it never deterred her, and I admit I looked on her with enormous respect - of the kind one gives to the Headteacher in a well-disciplined school! One did not argue with Miss Inglis! - nor did one cancel a booking unless they were 'deid or dyin'! She was officially the Secretary and all that entailed, which she did most efficiently. She also looked after the visiting mediums, attending to all their needs, shopping and cooking for them. She cleaned single handedly all 3 floors and the basement, and when she was not doing the hundred and one things which she took upon herself, she was to be heard playing the magnificent grand piano which stood in the lounge. This she did most beautifully, as she was the organist at The Church of Scotland Pathhead Church, staying in the same area, and travelling to and from The College on a regular basis, by local transport. Miss Inglis was a devout Christian, always maintaining that her church was where she practised her religion, whereas, in keeping with the constitution of The College, religion should be kept firmly outside. I sometimes wonder what she and the other founder members of The College would think of the mediums today who insist of praying in public from the platform! No longer politically correct of course.

But of course she was only one, there have been many fine souls who have gone into the building of this fine place, too many to write about, even if I could remember their names. All who worked willingly and voluntarily, cleaning, cooking, answering phones, looking after the mediums, etc. Perhaps some of you may recall the late Betty Smith, who gave of a large part of her life to the College. Due to lack of material goods in her life, she passed many an hour at the College generally helping out, but also reading. I recall the time when she took control of our wonderful library amongst her other 'wee jobs'. As you can imagine she became increasingly knowledgeable about Spiritual and Psychic 'things' and one day a young man asked her to recommend a book on a particular subject. When she recommended a particular book he commented laughingly, "Mrs Smith, have you read every book in this Library?" to which she replied, after some thought, "No dear, there are one or two I've not read yet!"

Two names out of hundreds, but the other thing I remember about Betty was that she always worried about The College! ALWAYS! She worried about the continuation of The College, mainly due to the constant in-fighting and power-mongering, the threats and resignations and sadly the unspiritual negativity that can so often be prevalent. Sadly those things are a fact of life and The College has never been immune to them but The College is a POWER SOURCE. Power of such immeasurable strength that it cannot be destroyed. Spirit set it up all these years ago and no matter how many problems there are, it will always survive. Spirit is life and life is indestructible; you can dent it and bruise it, you can bring it to its knees, but it will always survive. A Power greater than any of us can even imagine has decreed thus.

There will always be changes, people will come and go; no one is indispensable, that is the way of the world. THE ONLY CONSTANT IN LIFE IS CHANGE, that is true; we may accept that, we may not like it, but it is a fact.

This wonderful place, The Edinburgh College of Parapsychology, which to me will always be The Edinburgh Psychic College and Library, is, quite simply, meant to be and irrespective of Betty Smith's fears, it will always survive to help those who are in need - and what better purpose?

Today The Edinburgh College of Parapsychology is a vastly different place than The Psychic College and Library I grew up with all those years ago. Then, its core was Mediumship - bringing comfort to the bereaved; founded in 1932 to support life through a second world war and onwards. To-day it is a centre of foresight and Spiritual strength, offering seemingly unlimited opportunities towards greater understanding. Classes, Workshops, Talks on just about everything associated with Spiritual activity. An enormous emphasis on Healing, which is invaluable in today's world, where sadly 'stress' is the norm! Spiritual Healing is enormously successful in this particular field.

But none of that can be achieved without those wonderful souls who give of themselves to provide facilities for it all to happen. We today are better educated, no longer happy to be dictated to, we want to find out for ourselves, about ourselves and the possibilities of learning on a higher level; we are curious about the continuation of life after death and what this knowledge offers. Unfortunately not everyone has the advantage of my background, where knowledge of Spirit in my life was normal but The College gives you the opportunity to-find out, to bring to the fore hidden talents and find your true potential. This is where The College can and does help. It is not restricted by religious dogma; it opens its doors to all irrespective of creed.

The College has been a major part of my life, for which I will ever be grateful - I hope it has been and will be a major part of yours. Bear in mind, 1932 or 2007 'The structure is the same, just the bricks are different'.

As Miss Mae Inglis said to me all these years ago "Never Underestimate the Power of Spirit"

Spirit set up The College and I am enormously proud to be one of its children and the opportunities it has brought me. Let it bring them to you too.

75 Years is a long time - but merely a footprint in life. Quite simply - some things are meant to be, worked out by a Cosmic pattern too big for us to understand - and The College is part of that pattern - of THAT I am certain!

Nita Saunders

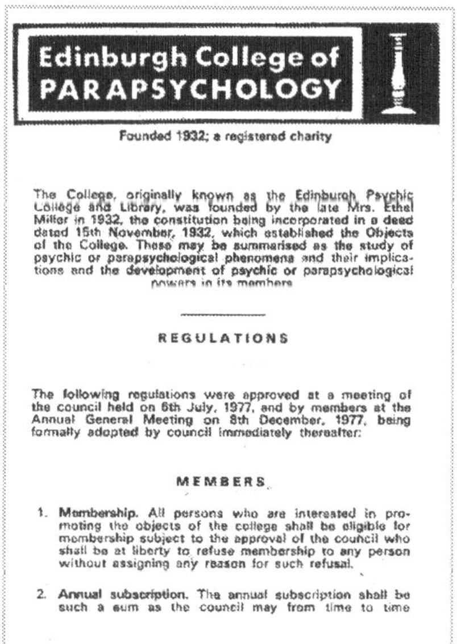

Edinburgh College of PARAPSYCHOLOGY

Founded 1932; a registered charity

The College, originally known as the Edinburgh Psychic College and Library, was founded by the late Mrs. Ethel Miller in 1932, the constitution being incorporated in a deed dated 15th November, 1932, which established the Objects of the College. These may be summarised as the study of psychic or parapsychological phenomena and their implications and the development of psychic or parapsychological powers in its members

REGULATIONS

The following regulations were approved at a meeting of the council held on 6th July, 1977, and by members at the Annual General Meeting on 8th December, 1977, being formally adopted by council immediately thereafter:

MEMBERS

1. **Membership.** All persons who are interested in promoting the objects of the college shall be eligible for membership subject to the approval of the council who shall be at liberty to refuse membership to any person without assigning any reason for such refusal.

2. **Annual subscription.** The annual subscription shall be such a sum as the council may from time to time

A copy of the Regulations of the College which were laid down in 1977.

Edinburgh College of PARAPSYCHOLOGY

Founded 1932, a registered charity.

2 Melville Street, Edinburgh EH3 7NS

Telephone 031-220 1433

PROGRAMME OF EVENTS
OPEN TO PUBLIC

ENQUIRIES from members of the public are INVITED

Encouragement and support is welcomed from NEW MEMBERS

(Membership £12 p.a.)

Office hours: 10 a.m. to 4 p.m.
Tuesday to Friday
Lunch 12.30 p.m. - 1.00 p.m.

Left:- One of the few records of events found for the 1980s.

Below:- Inside the Programme of Events. A year's Calendar from August 1985 to June 1986 showing the mediums who were booked for the 11 months for the Evidence of Survival Programme.

EVIDENCE OF SURVIVAL PROGRAMME

Programme for August, 1985, to July, 1986

Wednesday Demonstrations, 2.30 p.m.			Friday Demonstrations, 7.15 p.m.	
August	7	Mr John Edgar, Kilwinning	August	9
,,	14	Mr Gerard Smith, Burton	,,	16
,,	21	Mrs Lexie Findlater, Grangemouth	,,	23
,,	28	Mrs Ruby Webster, Cleveland	,,	30
September	4	Mr Gordon McKeown, Alloa	September	6
,,	11	Mrs Anita Sayle, Merseyside	,,	13
,,	18	Mrs Nessie Porter, Barrhead	,,	20
,,	25	Mr Albert Best, Glasgow	,,	27
October	2	Mrs Helen Wilson, Edinburgh	October	4
,,	9	Mr Ray Williamson, Stockport	,,	11
,,	16	Mr Les Driver, Rotherham	,,	18
,,	23	Mrs Ruby Grey, Wallsend	,,	25
,,	30	Mrs Clem Harvey, Glasgow	November	1
November	6	Mrs Nita Saunders, Edinburgh	,,	8
,,	13	Mr Gordon, McKeown, Alloa	,,	15
,,	20	Mrs Irene Leedham, Staffs.	,,	22
,,	27	Mrs Lexie Findlater, Grangemouth	,,	29
December	4	Mrs Jean Lamont, Alloa	December	6
,,	11	Mrs Mary Duffy, Edinburgh	,,	13
,,	18	Mrs Nessie Porter, Barrhead	,,	20
January	8	Mrs Helen Wilson, Edinburgh	January	10
,,	15	Mrs Clem Harvey, Glasgow	,,	17
,,	22	Mr Gordon McKeown, Alloa	,,	24
,,	29	Mrs Gerrard, Kirkcaldy	,,	30
February	5	Mrs Lexie Findlater, Grangemouth	February	7
,,	12	Mrs Nessie Porter, Barrhead	,,	14
,,	19	Mrs Nita Saunders, Edinburgh	,,	21
,,	26	Mrs Ann Holmes, Newcastle	,,	28
March	5	Mrs Irene Leedham, Staffs.	March	7
,,	12	Mrs Margaret Pearson, Scarborough	,,	14
,,	19	Mrs Jean Lamont, Alloa	,,	21
April	9	Mrs Clem Harvey, Glasgow	April	11
,,	16	Mr Bill Landis, London	,,	18
,,	23	Mrs Nessie Porter, Barrhead	,,	25
,,	30	Mrs Anita Sayle, Merseyside	May	1
May	7	Mrs Mary Duffy, Edinburgh	,,	9
,,	14	Mr Gordon McKeown, Alloa	,,	16
,,	21	Mrs Dorothy Patten, Guildford	,,	23
,,	28	Mrs Ruby Grey, Wallsend	,,	30
June	4	Mrs Nessie Porter, Barrhead	June	6
,,	11	Mrs Lexie Findlater, Grangemouth	,,	13
,,	18	Mrs Nita Saunders, Edinburgh	,,	20
,,	25	Mrs Clem Harvey, Glasgow	,,	27

Admission charges at College [illegible]0p Wednesday and [illegible]0p Friday for non-members, members free. Announcements in Saturday's Evening News (under the heading Spiritualists). Office open Friday evening 7 - 7.30 and 9 - 9.30.

..... *and finally*

All you need is love....love is all you neeed.

This story is incomplete. It has been our privilege to be the chronicler and compiler and to have charted the triumphs and vagaries of fortune that have accompanied the College through 75 years. The College story is truly one to be proud of. The College has a rich history indeed and the College deserves an honoured place in the annals of British Spiritual and Psychic Development.

There were once many such institutions and Edinburgh's College has endured and served and indeed has proven to be a "tough old bird". This story is incomplete because (the Edinburgh Psychic College and Library) - the Edinburgh College of Parapsychology is well placed to flourish for another 75 years.

In the final analysis, the love that Robert and Ethel Miller shared became their testimonial. The widowed Ethel was prepared to use her resources to provide facilities for others to explore Man's Spiritual and Psychic nature. In so doing, Mrs Miller sought generously to serve. Her gift to us, and one which has endured for 75 years is the College of Parapsychology. That gift was inspired by love and now "Mrs Miller's Gift" to us is one of Love.

Appendix 1

Mediums and Speakers known to have worked at and for the College from 1932 to the present day.

This alphabetical list is of those who have worked at or for the College by invitation of the College Council. Every care has been taken to make the list as comprehensive as possible, however the College records are incomplete, especially for the 1980's. Please accept our apologies if your name is not listed.

* known to have worked at the College between 1932 & 1956

** known to have worked at the College between 1957 & 1971

Without* have worked at the College between 1972 and the present day

Sibylle Alexander
Stewart Alexander: Tr./Phys. Med.
Estelle Anderson**
Mary Armour
Lillian Ayres
Lilian Bailey: Trance/Clairvoy.*
Mr Baker: Healing*
Maurice Barbanell: Speaker *
Mrs K. Barkell:Trance/ Clairvoy.*
Jean Bassett
Mary Batten
Paul Beard
Marlene Bell
Albert Best**
John Blackwood
Richard Boddington: Speaker*
Mrs Bowler**
Betty Boyd
Mark Brandist
Alma Brown
Jenny Brown
Maureen Brown
J.A.T.Bryan
Lynda Buchan
Linda Bulloch
Mrs Cairnduff: Healing*
Pat Campbell
Shirley Chubb
Peter Close
Mrs C. Constable
Mr O. Crombie
Julian Crump
Geraldine Cummins: Tr./Spkr.*
Helen Cuthill
Glynis Dailly
Agnes Davies
Eileen Davies
Lord Dowding: Speaker*
Eamonn Downey
Rev.C. Drayton Thomas: Speaker*
Les Driver
Mary Duffy**

Helen Duncan: Materialisation*
John Edgar
Harry Edwards: Healing*
Diane Elliott
Rev Maurice Elliott: Speaker*
Carol Ellis
George Evans**
Margaret Falconer
Mr R Fairweather**
J. Arthur Findlay: Speaker*
Lexie Findlater**
Rita Flanigan
Gwen Flower**
Dr Nandor Fodor: Speaker*
Thelma Francis
Colin Fry: Clairvoyance/Trance
Shelia Foulger
Bill Gardiner
Eileen Garrett: Tr./ Clairvoy.*
Mrs Gerrard
Janette Gilchrist
Ivy Gilhespie**
Tony Gleason
Jean Glen
Maureen Goodfellow
Roberta Gordon
Mr C.Grant
Ruby Grey
W L Haig: Speaker*
Duchess of Hamilton: Speaker*
Violet Hamilton
Jill Harland
Bertha Harris: Tr./ Clairvoy.*
Tom & Ann Harrison: Speakers
Clem Harvey
Geoffrey Hayward
June & Patrick Herraghty
Mrs Nina Hewitt
Bess Hewitson**
Bridget Hickey: Graphologist
Ann Hodgkinson**
Clive Holland
Ann Holmes
Ray Howden**
Helen Hughes: Clairvoy./Trance*
Brian Inglis**
Betty Irving
Ivor James Psychic Artist
May Jennings**
Lorna Jones
Stan Jones
Mrs Kelly: Clairvoyance*
David Kennedy
Margaret Kerr
Tekla Khan
Miss Margaret Kidd QC: Spkr.*
Mary Kidd**
Mrs Kidd
Paul Lambillion
Jean Lamont
Bill Landis
Rita Lawrie
Horace Leaf*
Irene Leedham
James Leigh(ed.TwoWorlds) Spk*
Mrs S. Leigh: Direct Voice*
George Lethem(ed.Light) Spkr*
Winnie Lewis
Nan Livingstone**
Len Loban
Isobel Lockie
John Lovette**
James Lowe
Carole Lynne
Mrs Lyon: Healing*.
Mrs MacCullum (Gl): Dir.Voice *
Mrs MacCullum (Ed):Tr./Clvoy.*
Mrs M MacIntosh
Rev. D. Mackay,
Jack MacKay**
Josephine MacKenzie
Gordon Mackeown

April Mackie
Bruce Macmanaway**
Kim MacManus:
Catrina McNab
Beatrice McCaig
J.B. McIndoe: Spkr./Clairvoyance*
Angela McInnes
Mrs McPherson**
Sally McQueenie
Barbara Meilkejohn-Free
Nee Menzies**
Diane Mitchell
Cecily Moore**
Roy Morgan
Linda and Duncan Muir
J. Murphy
Margaret Murray
Mrs Evelyn Napier**
Margaret Nicholson
Graeme Nisbet
Ivy Northage: Transfiguration*
Ernest Oaten: Speaker*
Dorothy Patten
Margaret Pearson
Sydney Peters, M.P.: Speaker*
Agnes Porter**
Edith Potts: Tr./ Clairvoyance*
Stanley Poulton Tr./Clairvoyance*
Mrs M. Pratt
Margaret Pritchard Jones
William Redmond**
Betty Reeves
Mary Reynolds
Estelle Roberts: Tr./Clairvoy.*
Susan Robertson
Stewart Robinson
Mike & Sue Rowlands
Professor Archie Roy: Speaker **
Nita Saunders
Anita Sayle
Harold Sharp: Psychic Artist**
Nora Shaw
Rita Shelhorn
John Sherwin
Mrs Smith**
Gerard Smith
Matthew Smith
Raymond Smith: Trance
Shirley Smith
Estelle Stead: Speaker*
Simone St. Clair: Speaker*
Marie St Clair Stobart*
Mrs Stevenson(USA)*
Hannen Swaffer: Speaker*
Mrs EdithThomson*
Jean Thompson: Tr./Clairvoy.**
Reg Truslove
Ena Twigg: Tr./ Clairvoyance*
G.W. Tyrrell: Speaker*
HaroldVigurs*
Betty Wakeling**
Ruby Webster
Mrs F.C.Whitson,
Dr Carl Wickland: Speaker *
Anne Wiley
Val Williams
Ray Williamson
Armand Wilson**
Helen Wilson
Bernice Winstanley
Prof. W Wright

Abbreviations:-
Clairvoy./Clvoy.: -Clairvoyance.
Phys. Med.:- Physical Medium
Spk. / Spkr. :- Speaker
Tr.: - Trance

References

Chapter 1

1. *Spiritualism and British Society Between the Wars:* Jenny Hazelgrove, p16.
2. *Dead Men's Embers*, pps 30,61.
3 *Dead Men's Embers,* p55.
4. *Where are the Dead* 3rd ed.1875 'Fritz'. p31
5. *Dead Men's Embers,* Gerald O'Hara.
6. *Spiritualism and British Society Between the Wars:* Jenny Hazelgrove.p15
7. *Manual and Who's Who of Spiritualism and Psychic Research 1936*: James Leigh. p32.
8. *Spiritualism and British Society Between the Wars:* Jenny Hazelgrove.p34
9. *Two Worlds.*
10. Psychic News, 10Nov. 973: Maurice Barbanell, (*Editor's Inside Story*)
11. *Miracles in Modern Life*: Rev J. Lamond.
12. The Scotsman (report on the opening of the College). 9th Sept 1932

Chapter 2

1. Rev C. Drayton Thomas. writer of: *Life Beyond Death with Evidence* and other books:
2. Editor of 'Two Worlds' & compiler of '*Manual and Who's Who of..Sp..*'
3. Editor of '*Communication, A Text Book*'; '*Blue Island.*'
4. Author of '*Thirty years Among the Dead*'.

Chapter 3

1. *The Mediumship of Helen Hughes:* Bernard Upton.
2. *The Story of Helen Duncan:* Alan E. Crossley. opp.p33
3. *'Marjorie':* Laura Culme Seymour.
4. *My Greatest Story*: Hannen Swaffer. p220

5. *Death is her life* (re: Lilian Bailey): photo: Psychic News 29.12.1979.
6. *Principles of Spiritualism* (F/word re. Vigurs): photo: Psychic News
7. Obituary for Horace Leaf: Psychic News 24.4.1971
8. *Ena Twigg, Medium*: Twigg E with Brod R.H. p78. *Spiritualism Today*: M. Barbanell. pps 85,167. photo: Psychic News 26.2.1994
9. Photograph from *Blue Island:* rec. byWoodman P. & Stead E.
10. *'My Dead still live'* E.Myers. p126: photo Psy. News cutting (undated)
11. '*Ena Twigg, Medium*': ETwigg with R.H. Brod. p78
12. *Spiritualism today*: M. Barbanell. p121-122
13. *100 years of Spiritualism*: Jean Bassett.
14. Obituary for Harold Sharp. Psychic News 5.4.1980 (photo & text)

Chapter 4

1. *'Best' of Both Worlds:* Rosalind Cattenach. p43.
2. *Inspired by Spirit*: Colin Fry. Two Worlds Publishing Co.
3. A Trilogy, spiritually transcribed by Raymond Smith i.'*Nobody wants to listen'*; ii.*For Those who are willing to listen...* ; iii. *The Truth, The Whole Truth and nothing but the Truth.*
4. *Experiences of Trance, Physical Mediumship and Assoc. Phenomena Part1 & Part 2* (with CDs of extracts of séances): Katie Halliwell.
5. *Sense of Something Strange*: Archie Roy. Dog&Bone, Glasgow 1990.

Chapter 5

1. *Dead Men's Embers*: Gerald O'Hara. p98.
2. *The Case for Spirit Photography*: Arthur Conan Doyle. p94.
3. *Photographing the Spirit World*: C.Permutt. p34-35.
4. *The Case for Spirit Photography*: Arthur Conan Doyle. p94.
5. *Marjorie*: Laura Culme-Seymour : p36.
6. Noah's Ark Newsletter, March 1993: Chairman's report
7. '*Light*', Vol LVI: 21 May 1936, p327, Letter to the Ed. by Colin Evans.
8. *Broadcasting from beyond*: A. E. Perriman: p60-.
9. *Life after Death-Living Proof*: Tom Harrison. p 155.
10. *Séance Photography'* by Colin Evans: "Photography" January 1936.
11. *The Giant Book of the Supernatural*: Colin Wilson. p21-242.

Books, Journals & Papers Consulted

Armour Mary: *Helen Duncan*: Pembridge Publishing: London 2000

Barbanell Maurice: *The Case of Helen Duncan*: Psychic Book Club: London 1945

Barbanell Maurice: *This is Spiritualism*: Herbert Jenkins. London 1959

Barbanell Maurice: *Spiritualism Today*: Herbert Jenkins. London 1969

Barrow Logie: *Independent Spirits*: Routledge & Kegan Paul 1986

Bassett Jean: *100 years of National Spiritualism:* SNU London: 1990

Boddington H: *Materialisations:* Psychic Press Ltd: London 1938

Boddington H: *The University of Spiritualism*: Spiritualist Press: London 1947

Brealey G with Hunter K: *The Two Worlds of Helen Duncan:* Regency Press: London. 1985

Cattenach Rosalind: *'Best'of Both Worlds:* Pembridge Publishing: London 1999

Crossley Alan E.: *The Story of Helen Duncan:* CON-PSY Publications, Greenford, Middlesex

Culme-Seymour Laura: *Marjorie*: Arthur H. Stockwell: Ilfracombe Devon (un-dated)

Doyle A C: *The Case for Spirit Photography*: Hutchinson & Co London 1926?

ECP: *The History of the Edinburgh College of Parapsychology*: Edinburgh 1982 pamphlet

Fritz: *Where are the Dead:* Simpkin Marshall & Co London 1875

Garrett Eileen: *My life*: Psychic Book Club: London 1939

Halliwell Katie: *Experiences of Trance, Physical Mediumship and Assoc. Phenomena: Part 2* SNPP2006

Harrison Tom: *Life after Death-Living Proof*: SNPP. York: 2004

Hazelgrove Jenny: *Spiritualism and British Society Between the Wars:* Manchester Uni. Press. 200_.

Lamond, Rev J.: *Miracles in Modern Life*: Simpkin Marshall: Lond.1928

Lamont Peter: *The First Psychic*: Little, Brown London: 2005

Leigh James: *Manual and Who's Who of Spiritualism and Psychic Research 1936*: Mott and Co, London 1936

Myers Erica: *My Dead Still Live*: Arthur Stockwell Ltd Devon 1961

Neech W F: *Death is her Life*:(story of Lilian Bailey): Psychic Press 1957

O'Hara Gerald: *Dead Men's Embers:* SNPP: York; 2006

Perriman A E: *Broadcasting from Beyond*: Psychic Press: London 1952

Permutt C: *Photographing the Spirit World:* Aquarian Press, Northants 1988

Spiritualist National Union: Year Book 2007: Stansted Essex

Stead Estelle (ed.): *Communication with Next World (A Text book)*: given by W.T.Stead. Cricket: London 1937

Swaffer Hannen: *Northcliffe's Return:* Psychic Book Club: London 1939

Swaffer Hannen: *My Greatest Story*: Psychic Book Club: London 1945

Twigg E with Brod R.H: *Ena Twigg Medium*: W H Allen.London. 1974

Two Worlds: *Photograph Album*: Manchester: circa 1900

Upton Bernard: *The Mediumship of Helen Hughes*: Spiritualist Press Ltd : 1945

Vigurs Harold: *The Principles of Spiritualism*: Headquarters Pub.CoLtd. London 1984

Wilson Colin: *The Giant Book of the Supernatural:* Parragon Book Service. Bristol 1995

Woodman P. & Stead E. (rec'd by): *The Blue Island:* Hutchinson & Co. London (undated)

Journals & Newspapers

Light

Noah's Ark Newsletter

Photography

Psychic News

Psychic World

The Edinburgh Evening Dispatch

The Manchester Guardian

The Scotsman

Two Worlds

The Authors

Gerald O'Hara was born in Middlesbrough in 1951 and educated to secondary school level in Redcar, Cleveland. Having travelled widely throughout the 70s, in 1979 he graduated from the London School of Economics in Sociology. Gerald has had a life long love of history and 'Mrs Miller's Gift' is his second book, having published 'Dead Men's Embers' in collaboration with Ann Harrison in 2006. He has been involved in the Spiritualist movement for 25 years and is the current President of the York Spiritualist Centre. Gerald lives in York and you may contact him on:
cargillohara@talk21.com

Ann Harrison was born, educated and lived for almost 60 years in the East Riding of Yorkshire before moving to the Alicante region of Spain, in 2000. She graduated from the University of Wales with a degree in Education and taught in primary schools for some years until the death of her first husband in 1990. His 'spirit return' introduced her to Spiritualism and through this she met her present husband Tom Harrison in 1993. Having setting up their own publishing company, Ann turned to an 'on-line' Printer to get Tom's book into print in 2004 and since then she has published 5 books and is Publications Editor for the international ITC Journal, which is issued in English/Spanish/Portuguese 3 times a year.

Ann may be contacted on: snppbooks@yahoo.co.uk

Index

NOTES

Lightning Source UK Ltd.
Milton Keynes UK
UKOW07f1858050215

245785UK00009B/266/P

9 780951 453490